A TEACHER'

*Pocket
Guide to
School Law*

A TEACHER'S

Pocket Guide to School Law

THIRD EDITION

Nathan L. Essex
Southwest Tennessee Community College
University of Memphis

Boston Columbus Indianapolis New York San Francisco Upper Saddle River
Amsterdam CapeTown Dubai London Madrid Milan Munich Paris Montreal Toronto
Delhi Mexico City São Paulo Sydney Hong Kong Seoul Singapore Taipei Tokyo

Vice President and Editorial Director: Jeffery W. Johnston
Senior Acquisition Editor: Meredith J. Fossel
Editorial Assistant: Janelle Criner
Vice President, Director of Marketing: Margaret Waples
Senior Marketing Manager: Darcy Betts
Program Manager: Laura Messerly
Project Manager: Jennifer Gessner
Development Project Management: Aptara®, Inc.
Procurement Specialist: Michelle Klein

Senior Art Director: Jayne Conte
Media Project Manager: Noelle Chun
Cover Designer: Karen Noferi
Cover Art: Fotolia
Full-Service Project Management: Munesh Kumar/Aptara®, Inc.
Composition: Aptara®, Inc.
Printer/Binder: LSC Communications
Cover Printer: LSC Communications, Inc. /North Chelmsford
Text Font: Minion Pro

Credits and acknowledgments for material borrowed from other sources and reproduced, with permission, in this textbook appear on the appropriate page within the text.

Every effort has been made to provide accurate and current Internet information in this book. However, the Internet and information posted on it are constantly changing, so it is inevitable that some of the Internet addresses listed in this textbook will change.

Library of Congress Cataloging-in-Publication Data
Essex, Nathan L., author.
  A teacher's pocket guide to school law / Nathan L. Essex, Southwest Tennessee Community College, University of Memphis.—Third edition.
    p. cm.
  ISBN-13: 978-0-13-335191-0
  ISBN-10: 0-13-335191-2
  1. Educational law and legislation—United States—Handbooks, manuals, etc. 2. School management and organization—United States. I. Title.
  KF4119.85.E85 2015
  344.73′071—dc23

                                                                2013028599

ISBN 13: 978-0-13-335191-0
ISBN 10:   0-13-335191-2

18 2021

*Dedicated to my spouse, Lorene,
and my children, Kimberly,
Jarvis, and Nathalie*

Contents

APPENDIX *A*

APPENDIX *B*

List of Cases

Preface

Teachers face numerous challenges in public schools. They are expected to exhibit excellence in teaching using best practices, to manage their classrooms effectively, to control student behavior, and to protect the health and safety of their students. The manner in which teachers perform these important duties may determine whether legal challenges will emerge. How, then, do teachers respond to legal problems they might encounter as they perform their important duties of teaching, supervising, and protecting the safety of students under their supervision? How do they know that their actions are not depriving students of their constitutional rights? How do teachers know when they are operating within the boundaries of the law? How do they demonstrate fundamental fairness in their dealings with students? *A Teacher's Pocket Guide to School Law,* Third Edition, is based on the premise that public school teachers must know the law that governs the organization and operation of schools in which they are employed.

Educators currently operate in a highly litigious society; they are constantly challenged by students and parents on a variety of issues surrounding their schools. Thus, teachers, as professionals, need to exercise discretion in making sound and legally defensible decisions that affect students under their care. The goal of this book is to provide comprehensive yet succinct and practical knowledge regarding relevant legal issues that affect teachers in public schools. The text includes a thorough discussion of the legislation that controls public schools and how such control affects public school teachers. After briefly covering landmark court cases that have shaped administrative practices in public schools, the book then covers areas such as religion, student rights, teacher freedoms, student and faculty disabilities, tenure, dismissal, and the use of social media, among other topics.

One salient feature of this text is its focus on school safety and the rights of students to due process in cases involving discipline. Tables and charts are carefully integrated into the text to amplify concepts and topics.

NEW TO THIS EDITION

The intent of the revisions in this Third Edition is to provide teachers with more in-depth information about the legal issues that affect them as they perform their duties and fulfill their responsibilities in public schools. Awareness of emerging and current legal issues will equip teachers with essential knowledge that will allow them to operate within the boundaries of educational law, thereby enabling them to avoid legal challenges as they execute their essential duties in an effective manner. This edition will ensure that teachers possess the necessary legal knowledge to enable them to function effectively.

The Third Edition includes the following additions and revisions:

CONTROL OF PUBLIC SCHOOLS

- An expanded section on local school boards that provides a comprehensive discussion of all dimensions of school board operations.
- An added section on discretionary powers of local school boards that describes the latitude granted school boards.
- An added section on the local school administrator's role in leading schools that defines their duties and responsibilities in contributing to positive student learning outcomes.

Instruction and Curriculum Standards

- The addition of a table of comprehensive guidelines covering all aspects of the Copyright Act that relate to teaching and instruction, including permissible and impermissible activities regarding fair use of copyright materials.

No Child Left Behind

- Identification of states as well as various subgroups that have received waivers. Requirements for waivers are included to facilitate greater understanding of significant components of the act.

- An added section on NCLB subgroups and the requirements they must meet in collecting and reporting assessment data.

Students, the Law and Public Schools

- An expanded section on viewpoint discrimination that provides guidance regarding permissible and nonpermissible restrictions on students' rights to freedom of expression.
- An expanded section on the position of the courts regarding the latitude that schools may or may not be granted in initiating student searches using canines.
- An expanded section on the types of dress that may be regulated by school or district policy student attire with examples of clothing worn by students that draws attention to the anatomy.

Due Process and Student Safety

- An added section on bullying in public schools to emphasize the inherent challenges teachers face in monitoring and controlling harassing and humiliating acts committed by students toward victims as well as liability challenges that may arise based on failure to respond to reports of bullying.
- An added section on cyberbullying in response to increased use of social media by students and the inherent damage to students who are victims of this type of undesirable behavior, as well as liability challenges that may arise when school personnel do not respond to these incidents.
- An added section on violence in public schools with recent statistics that illustrate the magnitude of the problem faced by school leaders and their faculties.
- A revised section on zero tolerance practices with examples of restrictions placed on students in conjunction with such policies.
- The addition of new guides on student suspension.

Teacher and School Liability

- An added section on parent chaperones and liability challenges they may face for negligence involving student supervision on field trip excursions.

Individuals with Disabilities

- An added section on multi-year IEPs, including the criteria the 15 approved states must meet to participate in the initiative, which eliminates annual reviews.

Discipline of Minority Students

- An added section on nationwide disparities involving discipline of minority students, as well as the potential legal ramifications of disparate treatment of students based on race and ethnicity.

Teachers and Ethical Behavior

- An added section on ethical behavior emphasizing the high standards of professional conduct teachers are expected to meet.

Transgender Teachers in Public Schools

- An added section on transgender teachers emphasizing teachers' freedom of choice in the context of fair treatment in the school environment, as well as their right to expect protection against gender discrimination as they fulfill their roles in public schools.

Use of Facebook and Social Media by Public School Teachers

- An added section on the use of Facebook and other social media that emphasizes the rights of students to freedom of expression within the context of acceptable and appropriate communication, as well as the responsibilities of teachers to be discreet in their use of such media, since teachers are considered by the courts as role models for students.

Religious Garb and Public Schools

- An expanded section on religious garb, with examples, that discusses teachers' religious freedoms as well as restrictions regarding their religious dress in public schools. The courts' position on this matter is also presented.

HIV-Positive Teachers in Public Schools

- An added section on the rights of HIV-positive teachers to teach if they pose no safety risk to students or colleagues, with an emphasis on the rights of HIV-positive teachers to be protected from discrimination based on their illness.

Collective Negotiations in Public Schools

- An added figure depicting the status of collective nego-tiations nationwide, designating states that provide coverage for all employees and states that do not, which may assist teachers with employment decisions based on this issue.
- An added map illustrating the status of charter schools in the United States.

Copyright Law and Teachers

- A revised, more comprehensive table on copyright and fair use that covers all aspects of the Copyright Act affecting teachers.

Court Cases

- The addition of relevant court cases throughout the text to provide greater guidance for teachers on the impact of court rulings on school operations.

Unique features of the book are the guides and practical tips covering an array of major issues faced by teachers. These are designed to assist school personnel, especially novice teachers, in achieving success in their employment positions. Guides and practical tips provide readers pertinent information to direct their day-to-day decisions as they face a wide range of legal challenges within their schools. The book concludes with appendices that include relevant constitutional provisions, carefully selected annotated federal statutes, and an abbre-viated glossary of important legal terms to assist the reader and provide relevant background. *A Teacher's Pocket Guide to School Law,* Third Edition, provides a practical and useful resource guide for teachers and other school professionals to increase their knowledge and understanding of the complex legal issues affecting their organizations. This resource will enable preservice teachers, in-service teachers, college and university teachers, education faculty and supervisors, policy makers, and central office supervisors in public schools to per-form their respective duties efficiently and effectively within the boundaries of constitutional, statutory, and case law.

ACKNOWLEDGMENTS

I would like to express my sincere appreciation to my administrative assistant, Carol Brown, for the countless hours spent preparing this document. Her relentless energy, enthusiasm, encouragement, and support far exceeded my expectations. For her untiring efforts, I am eternally grateful.

For their helpful comments, thanks to the following reviewers: Boyd Bradbury, Minnesota State University–Moorhead; Darlene Bruner, University of South Florida; Mark Sidelnick, University of North Carolina at Asheville; George Woodrow, University of North Texas–Dallas; Stuart Yager, Western Illinois University.

I would also like to express my appreciation to my family for their love, support, and encouragement during the writing of this text. Their support provided me inspiration to persevere through the completion of this project.

I convey my gratitude to Nathalie Essex, attorney-at-law, for her expert editorial and technical assistance, which aided me greatly in the production of this text.

Last, I express appreciation to my administrative team, friends, and colleagues for their support and encouragement during the writing of this new edition.

To my staff, colleagues, and family, I am immensely grateful.

About the Author

Nathan L. Essex is professor of Educational Administration in the College of Education at the University of Memphis and President of Southwest Tennessee Community College. He received a B.S. degree in English at Alabama A&M University, an M.S. degree in Educational Administration at Jacksonville State University, and a Ph.D. degree in Administration and Planning at The University of Alabama.

Essex's interests include law, educational policy, and personnel administration. He has served as consultant for more than 100 school districts and numerous educational agencies. He served as a policy consultant with the Alabama State Department of Education for 12 years and received numerous awards in recognition of his contributions in the field of education. He is the recipient of the Truman M. Pierce Award for Educational Leadership and outstanding contributions, which advanced the direction of education in the state of Alabama; the Academic Excellence Award, in recognition of professional achievement and academic excellence at the Capstone College of Education Society, University of Alabama; Teaching Excellence Award, The University of Alabama; Distinguished Service Award—Who's Who in the State of Tennessee and The University of Memphis Distinguished Administrator of the Year, 1995–96; and Alpha Beta Gamma's National Community College President of the Year, to name a few.

Essex has published numerous articles, book chapters, and newsletters on legal issues. His works appear in *The Administrator's Notebook, The Horizon, Compensation Review, The Clearinghouse, The American School Board Journal, Education and the Law, The School Administrator,* and other professional journals.

Introduction

The United States is a nation grounded in law, and public schools operate within the boundaries of established law. Public school law covers a wide array of subject matter that directly affects the organization and administration of public schools. Consequently, school officials must know the law and its impact on the daily operation of schools. Whereas a significant body of law relates specifically to education, a greater body of law regulates the operation of government. Because education is a function of state government, these laws directly affect public school systems.

Enacted law is derived from federal and state constitutions, as well as from federal and state statutes. Common law, or case law, the most prevalent source of legal authority, is derived from court decisions. Judicial decisions play a significant role in the management and operation of public schools. Decisions by the courts frequently alter school district policies and practices. Therefore, it is incumbent on educators and school officials to know the law and to operate within the parameters established by case law. For example, parental rights and responsibilities involving their children, tort liability, and essentials of contracts are based on common-law doctrine.

Law reflects the social and political patterns of society. Thus, court decisions should be examined in the context of the prevailing social and political climate that existed when the decision was rendered. Additionally, some courts are liberal, whereas others are conservative in their rulings, depending on their composition. Additionally, law is a dynamic field of study that requires school personnel to remain current in developments that affect the operation of schools.

Because school law is a generic field of study that covers a broad range of subject matter, it is vitally important that school personnel be well versed in the basic legal concepts supporting school law and be able to apply legal concepts to practices in public schools.

Chapter 1 provides the legal framework within which public schools operate and includes sources of law such as the federal and state constitutions, federal and state statutes, and the U.S. system of courts. Emphasis is placed on the important role these sources play in shaping policies, rules, and regulation for the operation of public schools.

Chapter 2 covers instruction and curriculum issues, as well as federal statutes that affect the instructional program. School vouchers and charter schools are also discussed, along with academic prerogatives involving teachers.

Chapter 3 addresses religion in public schools. The chapter identifies religious issues that bear on public schools, with an emphasis on the separation of church and state, the principle of neutrality, and the basic tenets of the First Amendment with respect to religious rights and freedoms of students.

Chapter 4 provides an overview of the constitutional rights of students in public schools and the relationship between school personnel and students with respect to student freedoms. Emphasis is placed on the need for reasonableness in the making of school rules and regulations pertinent to the personal rights and freedoms of students.

Chapter 5 includes a focused discussion of the due process rights of students, in the context of establishing safe schools where teachers can teach and students can learn. Gang violence is discussed, including measures that school personnel may take to minimize violence in public schools.

Chapter 6 covers the privacy rights of public school students and their parents. Measures are discussed that are necessary to protect the confidentiality of student records, as well as liability challenges involving defamation that may emerge when students' privacy rights are violated.

Chapter 7 addresses individuals with disabilities and the legal requirements that must be met regarding the educational needs of students with disabilities. Relevant issues involving placement, related services, and the due process rights of students with disabilities and their parents are discussed.

Chapter 8 provides a discussion of school liability and teachers' duties to protect students from foreseeable harm. Defenses to liability are discussed, as is liability based on failure to meet the proper standard of care in instructing and supervising students.

Chapter 9 addresses discrimination in employment issues and the rights that are afforded teachers under the Fourteenth Amendment with respect to fairness in the employment process. Federal statutes are discussed that provide protection against employment discrimination in public schools.

Chapter 10 covers the rights and freedoms to which public school teachers are entitled in the school environment, along with reasonable restrictions that school officials may place on teachers under certain conditions.

Chapter 11 discusses teacher employment issues involving tenure, dismissal, and collective negotiations, along with the legal requirements that are necessary to protect teachers. Property rights regarding tenure, due process provisions, and liberty interests involving untenured teachers are addressed.

1

Control of Public Schools

STATE AND LOCAL CONTROL OF EDUCATION

Public education is a federal interest, a state function, and a local responsibility. A federal interest is manifested through the passage of various federal statutes, such as Title I, Goals 2000, the Educate America Act of 1994, Education for Disabled Students, and No Child Left Behind, that affect the operation of public schools. These statutes are designed to create educational opportunities for students and to improve the quality of public education by creating greater accountability for achieving desired educational outcomes. The Tenth Amendment to the U.S. Constitution provides that the powers "not delegated to the United States by the Constitution nor prohibited by the Constitution to the states are reserved to the states respectively and to the people." Thus, by virtue of the Tenth Amendment, the control of education is vested in the states and the people. The responsibility for the operation and control of public schools resides with the state. Unless restricted by state constitutions, state legislatures have the authority to govern public schools. Most state constitutions refer to the legislature as maintaining responsibility for public education. Although the state legislature has ultimate control over public schools, its control is not unrestricted but is subject to review by state and federal courts to ensure that the constitutional rights of citizens are protected.

The state legislature has plenary power to establish schools and to develop a unique system of public schools. This legislative power was illustrated in a very early Michigan decision wherein the U.S. Supreme Court held that the legislature has entire control over the

- schools of the state,
- division of the states into districts,

- conduct of the schools, and
- qualifications of teachers.[1]

The subjects to be taught within each state are all within the state's control.[2] The power of the state to control education is derived from the state's police power, which presumes that the state is responsible for the health, safety, and welfare of its citizens. The police power of a state extends to the protection of the lives, limbs, health, comfort, and quiet of all persons and to the protection of all property within the state.[3] State legislatures have the authority to govern education, and this authority involves both the legislative and executive branches of government and includes regulations that promote domestic order, morals, health, and safety.[4]

Students who enroll in public schools are subject to state laws and local regulations governing the operation of public schools. The state's police powers provide the state the authority to control education, including such matters as requiring compulsory attendance and immunization for children attending public schools. The state's police powers allow it to formulate rules and regulations designed to protect the health, safety, and well-being of all citizens. It is within this context that children are provided a free public education. Local school boards are delegated responsibility for the daily operations of schools within their districts and are subject to federal and state laws and state board of education policy, as well as federal and state constitutional mandates. The local school board is responsible for formulating school district policy that enables the district to operate effectively and efficiently in achieving its goals. Thus, federal, state, and local entities have established the context for public education in the United States.

State Board of Education

State boards of education are generally established by the state legislature. Normally, members are elected by popular vote and represent respective districts throughout the state. The board is responsible for policy development, general supervision, and control of public schools throughout the state. The board also appoints the chief state school officer.

Chief State School Officer

The chief state school officer is probably the most influential professional educator within the state. Appointed by the state board of education to a set term, the chief state school officer is usually the chief executive officer of the board.

His or her primary duty is to execute the educational policies of the state board of education and oversee the operations of public schools within the state to ensure their compliance with state board policy.

State Department of Education

The state board of education is authorized by the legislature to employ, upon recommendation of the chief state school officer, the professionals necessary to execute the policies of the board to facilitate the effective operation of public schools throughout the state. Although there are variations among states, most state departments consist of divisions of administration and finance, federal programs, disability services, student services, academics, legislation, research and evaluation, charter schools, teacher and leader effectiveness, professional standards, audits, and management, among others. The department provides services and support to local school systems in virtually all aspects of local school district operations.

Local Control of Public Schools

Local school boards, created by state statute, are expected to execute state and federal laws and state board policy governing the operations of schools under their jurisdiction. They also raise revenue through tax levies and school bonds to construct and maintain facilities, and to purchase equipment, supplies, and other items essential to the operation of schools. Although school board members act as agents of the state, they represent the district electors, parents, citizens, and communities they serve.

School board members are considered to be state, not local, officials because the education function is categorized as one of statewide responsibility. Local school board members are generally elected or appointed and hold office by virtue of legislative enactment. The state legislature also prescribes their powers, which may be broadened or limited at the legislature's discretion. Local board members may be required to meet certain residency requirements to qualify for election or appointment to the board of education.

Local school boards exercise powers, either implied or specified, to manage school districts, including rendering decisions regarding curriculum, although the legal authority for defining the curriculum of public schools resides with the legislature. Based on constitutional provisions, in a few states this duty is shared between the legislature and the state board of education. The legislature may, at its discretion, prescribe the basic course of study and determine testing standards and graduation requirements. In most cases, state legislatures delegate curriculum matters to state boards of education and, most important, to local school districts. Local school boards are granted statutory powers that are essential to achieving their purpose. To a large degree local boards are delegated the authority to render decisions regarding curriculum and instruction within their districts, such as choosing and regulating curricula and course offerings, and determining curricula that are best suited for students. Local boards also make decisions regarding books and other educational tools including technology utilization. Based on delegated powers, many local school districts have established local school-based management councils that are empowered to make decisions in matters regarding curriculum and instructional practices, textbook selection, and choice of instructional materials. Local school boards are authorized to employ and dismiss personnel, construct buildings, and provide district-wide transportation.

The local board of education is the legal entity for school districts. The board acts as a corporate body. No single board member has authority outside that of the board as a whole. The local board of education is a policy-making body that has the responsibility to adopt policies and procedures for the organization and administration of schools within the district. School district policies are generally based on state statute. School leaders have the responsibility to execute these policies. The relationship between the board of education and its district leader is best described as a legislative–executive relationship. The board formulates policies, and the superintendent executes them. Because policies provide direction and guidance for teachers, it is imperative that teachers understand and adhere to policies that affect their professional duties. If the legality of a policy is challenged, the burden rests with the school district to defend its policy. However, lack of awareness of school and district policies does not protect teachers who commit policy violations. Teachers may be disciplined, based on the seriousness of the policy violation; penalties may include dismissal for acts that are contrary to board policy.

School boards may hold executive sessions to discuss sensitive matters such as employee discipline, contract issues, or consultation with attorneys. Only board members may attend these meetings. The intent of such meetings is to protect the confidentiality of sensitive information or of information that may damage a person's good name or reputation. Consequently, all items discussed during executive sessions are confidential and should not be divulged by board members.

Discretionary Powers

The school board may exercise discretionary powers based on its judgment and is restricted only by statutory requirements. Examples of discretionary powers include establishing the school calendar, purchasing school buses, determining the location of school buildings, and adopting a salary schedule that exceeds the state's minimum salary schedule.

School Administrator's Role

The role of the local school administrator may vary from school to school, but most administrators are responsible for the day-to-day operation of their school. One of their top priorities is evaluating the success of the instructional program as well as teacher performance and effectiveness. The school administrator in conjunction with teachers is responsible for maintaining a safe and orderly learning environment where teachers teach and students learn. Additionally, the administrator ensures that instructional and curricula goals are achieved. Supervision, evaluation, and support of faculty are critically important to achieving desired goals of the school. The school leader generates tenure and dismissal recommendations, allocates adequate resources to achieve the school's instructional goals, oversees school curricula and extracurricular activities, and serves as an ambassador for the school and the district.

Teachers as Employees of Local School Boards

School districts are public corporations. Teachers are public employees who are employed by local boards of education in a contractual relationship and are agents of the school district in which they are employed. The board of education is the only entity that has the legal authority to employ or dismiss school personnel. In some instances, principals recommend teachers for employment positions within their respective schools to the superintendent of schools, but these recommendations carry no legal standing until the board of education approves the superintendent's recommendation. The superintendent has the prerogative to accept or reject a principal's recommendation. The board may also reject the superintendent's recommendations as long as the rejection is nondiscriminatory and based on defensible criteria. Employment rejections that are arbitrary or capricious will not be upheld by the courts.

School District Rules and Regulations

Boards of education have the implied power to formulate and enforce rules and regulations necessary to facilitate the efficient operation of schools within the district. School board rules and regulations must be reasonable and consistent with state and federal constitutional provisions, but it is often difficult to determine the reasonableness of rules. The courts generally presume that the board's actions are reasonable. Since reasonableness is presumed, the burden of proof resides with the party who challenges board rules.

The presumption of reasonableness is established by the courts, based on the view that the role of the courts is not to make policy. However, the courts will not hesitate to review school rules and regulations when substantive challenges arise. A court will then determine whether the rules and regulations are arbitrary, capricious, or in violation of the constitutional rights of school personnel or students. A reasonable exercise of administrative authority will generally receive support by the courts.

School Board Meetings

School board meetings, as well as minutes of these meetings, are open to the public. Any citizens, including teachers, who desire to do so may attend board meetings. Most states have adopted "sunshine," or open-meeting, laws designed to ensure that the public is informed on matters of public interest. The only exception to open meetings occurs when the board meets in executive session to discuss matters pertaining to personnel issues and other sensitive legal subject matter.

GUIDES

Control of Public Schools

1. The federal government has an interest in public education through the enactment of statutes designed to improve education.
2. Public schools are state controlled by virtue of the Tenth Amendment to the U.S. Constitution.
3. The state legislature has complete authority to govern public schools, including, but not limited to, teacher

qualifications, curriculum matters, funding, and student graduation requirements.

4. Each state has police power, which creates a responsibility to protect the health, safety, and welfare of its citizens.

5. The power to control education is derived from the state's police powers.

6. School boards have specific or implied powers to administer schools within their districts.

7. Local school board members are considered to be state officers because education is a state function.

8. The school board as a policy-making entity has responsibility for guiding the district through development of legally defensible policies and procedures.

9. The local school board is the only entity that has the legal authority to employ or dismiss school personnel.

10. Teachers are public employees whose responsibilities are defined in a contractual relationship with the local school board.

11. Teachers have a leading responsibility to become familiar with and execute school or district policies, rules, and regulations.

12. Inadequate knowledge of policy is not a justifiable defense for teachers who violate policy.

13. Teachers may be disciplined, including being dismissed, for policy violations, according to the seriousness of the violation and its impact on the district.

PRACTICAL TIPS

Do:

1. Understand the rights and responsibilities associated with your teaching position. Awareness of your rights will provide guidance and direction and allow you to successfully execute your professional duties effectively.

2. Become familiar with school and district policies. Lack of knowledge will not provide relief from discipline for failure to perform your assigned duties and responsibilities.

3. Attend school board meetings periodically and become familiar with the issues and challenges faced by your district. Such familiarity may assist you in meeting district expectations successfully.

4. Understand your employment status as an agent of your school district, and understand the source of authority that you possess in your teaching position. Employment knowledge will allow you to operate within the boundaries of acceptable practice within your district.

Do not:

1. Ignore the governance structure of your school and district. It is necessary to follow the chain of command as you address issues and challenges that affect your employment position.
2. Violate school or district policies. Failure to adhere to these policies may form grounds for dismissal, depending on the consequences related to the violation.
3. Fail to recognize the type of behavior that is expected of teachers, who must exercise sensitivity regarding the professional image associated with teaching. Expectations may vary with the community in which you are employed.
4. Underestimate the importance of membership in local and national professional associations. They provide enormous benefits in all aspects of the teaching profession, including liability coverage.

ENDNOTES

1. *State of Michigan ex rel. Kies v Lowry*, 199 U.S. 233, 26 S. Ct. (1905).
2. *Child Welfare Society of Flint v. Kennedy School Dist.*, 220 Mich. 290, 189 N.W. 1002 (1922).
3. *Leeper v. State*, 103 Tenn. 500, 53 S.W. 962 (1899).
4. *Railroad Co. v. Husen*, 95 U.S. 465 (1877).

2

Instruction and Curriculum Standards

ACADEMIC ISSUES

Curriculum Standards

The term *curriculum* generally encompasses the range of courses taken by students, but in specific programs it also describes the teaching, learning, and assessment processes involved in a given course of study. Minimal curriculum standards in public schools are established by state statute. In almost all cases, certain courses and minimum achievement standards are determined through state statute, as well. Local school districts may establish other curriculum standards so long as they do not contradict state requirements. However, Article VI of the U.S. Constitution—the *Supremacy Clause*—specifies that all laws and treaties made by the federal government shall be the supreme law of the land. The supremacy clause allows the federal government to enact laws that prevail over conflicting or inconsistent state exercise of power. Thus, the federal government formulates l statutes that apply to public schools. For example, federal aid programs specify certain standards that states must meet to receive federal funds. Courts are very reluctant to intervene in matters involving public school curricula, on the basis that states retain the authority to establish curriculum standards as long as they do not infringe on federal statutes.

The legal authority for defining curriculum resides with the state legislature. In some states, this duty is shared between the legislature and the state board of education. The legislature may, at its discretion, prescribe the basic course of study, testing standards, and graduation requirements for students, as well as the testing standards for teachers. Virtually every state has developed academic standards to facilitate student achievement, and states are increasingly assuming responsibility for identifying the essential knowledge and skills that students must possess to become productive citizens. Supplemental services are provided by a number of states to assist students in meeting their academic needs. In fact, the Elementary and Secondary Education Act of 1965 (ESEA) requires that schools failing to make adequate progress for two consecutive years or more use a portion of their Title I funds to allow low-income students to enroll in supplemental services. This act is revised every 5 to 7 years. The eighth revision passed by Congress in 2001 and signed into law in 2002, the No Child Left Behind (NCLB) Act, was designed to close the achievement gap between disadvantaged and minority students and their peers and to create greater accountability in education.

NO CHILD LEFT BEHIND ACT OF 2001

On January 8, 2002, President George W. Bush signed NCLB into law. NCLB is considered to be the most sweeping reform since the ESEA was passed in 1965. The law technically expired in 2007 and the House recently voted to overhaul it and reverse some of its provisions. NCLB redefines the federal government's role in K–12 education and is based on four principles:

- stronger accountability for results,
- increased flexibility and local control,
- expanded options for parents, and
- an emphasis on teaching methods that have been proven to work.

Public School Choice

Public school choice, supplemental education services, and collective bargaining agreements fall under the accountability provisions in the Title I program. Under NCLB, each state must establish a definition of "adequate yearly progress" to determine the achievement of each school within the district and must identify for improvement any Title I school that fails to meet the state's definition of adequate yearly progress for two consecutive years or more. These schools, with technical assistance from their school districts, must develop and implement improvement plans incorporating various strategies to strengthen instruction in core academic subjects and address specific issues that contributed to the school's failure. These schools must also provide public school choice and supplemental education services.

Waivers have been granted to 32 states and to the District of Columbia. Eight of the 32 states have conditional status, meaning that they have not entirely satisfied the administration's requirements, and their plans are under review. In exchange for waivers, states had to agree to a plan that included parts of the Obama administration's proposal for reauthorizing ESEA—the College and Career-Ready Standards and Assessments—as well as grading teachers using students' standardized test scores as one criterion. Under this agenda, only 15% of each state's lowest performing schools would be penalized.

In general, a school district is required to provide all students enrolled in any Title I elementary or secondary school identified for improvement the option to transfer to another public school in the school district—which may include a public charter school that has not been identified for improvement. This choice requirement applies unless state law specifically prohibits it, according to a key policy letter from the secretary of education in 2002.

PUTTING READING FIRST

NCLB fully implements President Bush's Reading First initiative. The act is committed to ensuring that every child can read by the end of third grade. To accomplish this goal, the Reading First initiative is expected to significantly increase federal investment in scientifically based reading instruction programs in the early grades. This initiative is also expected to reduce the number of children identified for special education services due to a lack of appropriate reading instruction.

Summary and Implications

Increased Accountability

- **Increased Accountability for Ensuring Progress:** Each state will implement a statewide accountability system that will be effective in ensuring that all districts and schools make adequate progress. The accountability system includes rewards and sanctions.

- **Limitations on Leaving Students Behind:** Students cannot be left behind because of
  a. race or ethnicity,
  b. disabilities,
  c. limited English proficiency, or
  d. economic status (disadvantaged).
- **Increased Accountability for Student Performance:** States, districts, and schools that improve achievement will be rewarded. Failure will be sanctioned. Parents will know how well their child is learning. Schools are held accountable for their effectiveness with annual state reading and math assessments in grades 3–8.
- **A Focus on What Works:** Federal dollars will be spent on effective research-based programs and practices. Funds will be targeted to improve schools and enhance teacher quality.
- **Reduced Bureaucracy and Increased Flexibility:** Additional flexibility will be provided to states and school districts, and flexible funding will be increased at the local level.
- **Empowerment of Parents:** Parents will possess more information regarding the quality of their child's school. Students in persistently low-performing schools will be provided a choice to enroll in a high-performing school.

Participation

- Students with disabilities who undergo alternative assessment must participate in the assessment process.
- Up to 2% (approximately 20% of students with disabilities) of students with proficient and advanced scores from alternative assessment based on modified academic achievement standards may be included in calculating adequate yearly progress.
- Schools and districts must average a 95% participation rate for all students over a 2-year period.

Adequate Yearly Progress

- The same high academic achievement standards will be applied to all students.
- There should be continuous and demonstrated academic improvement for all students.
- Separate measures and annual achievement objectives may be used for all students, including students from all racial and ethnic groups, economically disadvantaged students, students with disabilities, and students with limited English proficiency.

Teacher Quality

- All core academic teachers were required to be highly qualified by 2005–6.
- Core academics includes
  a. English, reading, or languages;
  b. mathematics, science, foreign languages, civics, and government; and
  c. economics, arts, history, and geography.

Qualified Teachers

The following measures were used in part to assess qualified teachers:

- a teacher's license,
- a passing score on a test, and
- content area knowledge:
  a. academic major or graduate degree in content area,
  b. credits equivalent to academic major (24 hours), and
  c. a passing score on a test such as Praxis.

Paraprofessionals

Paraprofessionals must meet *one* of the following requirements:

- 2 years of higher education,
- an associate's degree,
- ParaPro Assessment (a competency measure for reading, writing, and math),
- a high school diploma or its equivalent.

Students

Each group of students should meet or exceed annual objectives, with the following exceptions:

a. There should be a 10% reduction from the prior year in the number of students who are below proficiency standards.
b. Other indicators may be used to measure progress for subgroups.

Restructuring (Corrective Action)

If a school fails to make adequate yearly progress after one full year of corrective action, the district must

a. continue to make public school choice available,
b. continue to make supplemental services available, and
c. prepare a plan to restructure the school.

Alternative Governance

By the beginning of the following school year, the district must implement *one* of the following alternatives:

a. reopen the school as a public charter school;
b. replace all or most of school staff, including the principal;
c. enter into a contract with an entity, such as a private management company with a proven record of effectiveness, to operate the school; or
d. submit to state takeover.

NCLB SUBGROUPS

Federal Data Requirements for Report Cards Under No Child Left Behind

Broadly speaking, all states and Local Education Agencies (LEAs) must collect and report information on their academic assessments in reading/language arts and math (and science beginning in 2007–8), Adequate Yearly Progress (AYP) results, and teachers' qualifications. Many of these data elements must be disaggregated by federally defined subgroups, necessitating the collection of student demographic information. A full discussion of federal NCLB Report Card requirements can be found in the nonregulatory guidance issued on September 12, 2003, by the U.S. Department of Education (at http://www.ed.gov/programs/titleiparta/reportcardsguidance.doc). Annual federal NCLB Report Card reporting requirements for Title I, Part A, recipients are summarized in the following table.

VOUCHERS

Although the use of government-administered vouchers has increased over the past two decades, they have not received strong support from public school teachers, parents, or the general public, particularly in cases where funds allocated for vouchers compete with public school funding. Educational funding channeled to families allows them to choose where their children will attend school. The theory behind vouchers is that parental choice will trigger competition between public and private schools, which will result in improved education for all children. Among the concerns of public school officials are that vouchers tend to create a heavy reliance on the government, and they generate additional regulations and governmental intervention in educational policy.

One of the High Court's arguments for choice in public education is the degree to which the public schools have already introduced elements of choice—international baccalaureate programs, magnet schools, "fundamental" schools, alternative schools, and charter schools. School districts in Milwaukee, Wisconsin, and Cleveland, Ohio, offer voucher programs. The Florida legislature has passed voucher legislation that, its proponents believe, will serve as a model throughout the nation. Dozens of other cities and states are actively engaged in debates on the subject.

In a significant ruling, the Supreme Court of Wisconsin held that the expanded Milwaukee voucher program, which allowed 15,000 children to attend any private school, including religious schools, does not violate either state or federal constitutions.[1]

CHARTER SCHOOLS

According to the U.S. Department of Education, charter schools are public schools that emerge through a contract with a state agency or a local school board. The charter establishes the ground rules regarding the operations of the school. The first charter school was created in Minnesota in 1992. Since then, 41 other states and the District of Columbia have established charter schools. The primary advantage of charter schools is autonomy over their operations; they are relieved of rules and regulations that govern other public schools. In exchange for flexibility, charter schools are held accountable for achieving outcomes established by the charter, which include student achievement as a primary goal. The charter school concept is sound. Proponents of charter schools suggest that they encourage innovation and creativity without bureaucratic barriers, in exchange for measurable and positive student learning outcomes. Charter schools have become more flexible in adapting to the educational needs of individual children. There are more than 5,600 charter schools across the country, educating over 2 million children. The charter school movement is considered to be dynamic and strong, with many successes, as well as ongoing challenges regarding facility problems, deregulation, state and local resistance, and inadequate funding. States with established charter schools are listed in Figure 2.1.

TABLE 2.1 Local-Level Student Achievement Data

An LEA must include the data elements associated with student achievement detailed below on its local report card. Except as otherwise indicated, the LEA must report student achievement data on the State's assessments in reading/language arts, mathematics, and science. The LEA must report this information for the LEA as a whole and for each school served by the LEA.

Data element	All Students	Major racial & ethnic groups	Students with disabilities[1]	English Learners (EL)[2]	Econ. disadvantaged	Migrant	Gender	Combined subgroups[3]
Participation Rate on State Assessments								
Percentage of students not tested for each subject assessed[4]	✓	✓	✓	✓	✓	✓	✓	✓
Number of recently arrived EL students exempted from the reading/language arts assessment				✓				
Student Achievement on State Assessments								
Student achievement at each academic achievement level for each subject assessed[5]	✓	✓	✓	✓	✓	✓	✓	✓
Most recent 2-year trend data in student achievement for each subject and grade level assessed	✓							

TABLE 2.1 *(continued)*

LEA achievement compared to State achievement	✓	✓	✓	✓
School achievement compared to LEA and State achievement	✓	✓	✓	
Student Achievement on State NAEP				
Percentage of students at each achievement level in the State on State NAEP in reading and mathematics for grades 4 and 8	✓			
Participation rates for EL students and students with disabilities in the State on State NAEP	✓	✓		

[1] Includes results for all students with disabilities under IDEA, including results on alternate assessments based on grade-level, modified, or alternate academic achievement standards. Does not include results for students covered under Section 504 of the Rehabilitation Act of 1973 but not covered by IDEA. Does not include former English Learners.

[2] Does not include former English Learners.

[3] Only relevant for LEAs in certain States that receive ESEA flexibility. An LEA in such State should identify what students comprise each combined subgroup.

[4] In the alternative, an LEA may report the percentage of students tested.

[5] An LEA must report student achievement data for each academic achievement level of the State assessment system and should use the academic achievement level "labels" associated with that system.

Source: State and Local Report Cards: Questions and Answers, U.S. Department of Education, February 28, 2013; http://www2.ed.gov/programs/titleiparta/rptcard2282013.pdf

FIGURE 2.1　States with charter schools.
(*Source:* © Copyright 2006–12, The National Alliance for Public Charter Schools. 1101 Fifteenth Street, NW, Suite 1010, Washington, DC 20005. (202) 289-2700. Use of this material is by permission of the publisher; http://publiccharters.org/.)

GUIDES

Instructional Program

1. The state legislature has a responsibility to provide schooling, at public expense, for all children within the state.
2. The legal authority for defining curriculum resides with the legislature.
3. Courts typically do not intervene in curriculum matters, because each state retains the authority to establish curriculum standards. The courts will intervene only if legitimate constitutional issues emerge.
4. All schools should be held accountable for ensuring that the achievement gap between disadvantaged or minority students and their peers is closed, under the NCLB Act.
5. Vouchers and charter schools are designed to improve student achievement by providing choices for students and parents.

INTELLECTUAL PROPERTY AND FAIR USE

Intellectual property covers four basic areas: patents, trademarks, designs, and copyrighted materials. The Copyright Act of 1976 prohibits unauthorized use of copyrighted material for profit or public display without appropriate payment to or permission from the copyright proprietor. Under the act, the owner of a copyright has the exclusive rights to do and to authorize any of the following:

1. to reproduce the copyrighted work in copies or phonorecords;
2. to prepare derivative works based upon the copyrighted work;
3. to distribute copies or phonorecords of the copyrighted work to the public by sale or other transfer of ownership or by rental, lease, or lending;
4. in the case of literary, musical, dramatic, and choreographic works, pantomimes, and motion pictures and other audiovisual works, to perform the copyrighted work publicly; and
5. in the case of literary, musical, dramatic, and choreographic works, pantomimes, and pictorial, graphic, or sculptural works, including the individual images of a motion picture or other audiovisual work, to display the copyrighted work publicly.

The Copyright Act specifies four factors that should be used to determine fair use:

1. purpose or use relative to whether use is commercial in nature or for nonprofit, educational purposes;
2. nature of the work;
3. amount of material extracted from the work in relation to the work as a whole; and
4. impact of the use on the potential market in relation to the value of the copyrighted work.[2]

Copying Computer Software

Copyright laws also affect computer software. Teachers should not reproduce copies of software for students from an original program to serve as a backup copy, because such reproduction is prohibited under the Copyright Act. Most school districts purchase site licenses to provide legal protection for the use of software. This license is a contractual agreement with a software company that allows use of educational software for a negotiated fee. Under the contractual agreement, a reasonable number of copies may be reproduced for educational purposes. Laws also apply to the use of copyrighted multimedia. Table 2.2 provides information regarding fair use.

TABLE 2.2 Copyright and Use of Media

Copyright and Fair Use Guidelines for Teachers

TECHNOLOGY *and* LEARNING

This chart was designed to inform teachers of what they may do under the law. Feel free to make copies for teachers in your school or district, or download a PDF version at www.techlearning.com. More detailed information about fair use guidelines and copyright resources is available at www.halldavidson.net.

Medium	Specifics	What you can do	The Fine Print
Printed Material (short)	• Poem less than 250 words; 250-word excerpt of poem greater than 250 words • Articles, stories, or essays less than 2,500 words • Excerpt from a longer work (10 percent of work or 1,000 words, whichever is less) • One chart, picture, diagram, or cartoon per book or per periodical issue • Two pages (maximum) from an illustrated work less than 2,500 words, e.g., a children's book	• Teachers may make multiple copies for classroom use, and incorporate into multimedia for teaching classes. • Students may incorporate text into multimedia projects.	• Copies may be made only from legally acquired originals. • Only one copy allowed per student. • Teachers may make copies in nine instances per class per term. • Usage must be "at the instance and inspiration of a single teacher," i.e., not a directive from the district. • Don't create anthologies. • "Consumables," such as workbooks, may not be copied.
Printed Material (archives)	• An entire work • Portions of a work • A work in which the existing format has become obsolete, e.g., a document stored on a Wang computer	• A librarian may make up to three copies "solely for the purpose of replacement of a copy that is damaged, deteriorating, lost, or stolen."	• Copies must contain copyright information. • Archiving rights are designed to allow libraries to share with other libraries one-of-a-kind and out-of-print books.
Illustrations and Photographs	• Photograph • Illustration • Collections of photographs • Collections of illustrations	• Single works may be used in their entirety, but no more than five images by a single artist or photographer may be used. • From a collection, not more than 15 images or 10 percent (whichever is less) may be used.	• Although older illustrations may be in the public domain and don't need permission to be used, sometimes they're part of a copyright collection. Copyright ownership information is available at www.loc.gov or www.mpa.org.
Video (for viewing)	• Videotapes (purchased) • Videotapes (rented) • DVDs • Laserdiscs	• Teachers may use these materials in the classroom. • Copies may be made for archival purposes or to replace lost, damaged, or stolen copies.	• The material must be legitimately acquired. • Material must be used in a classroom or nonprofit environment "dedicated to face-to-face instruction." • Use should be instructional, not for entertainment or reward. • Copying OK only if replacements are unavailable at a fair price or in a viable format.
Video (for integration into multimedia or video projects)	• Videotapes • DVDs • Laserdiscs • Multimedia encyclopedias • QuickTime Movies • Video clips from the Internet	• Students "may use portions of lawfully acquired copyrighted works in their academic multimedia," defined as 10 percent or three minutes (whichever is less) of "motion media."	• The material must be legitimately acquired (a legal copy, not bootleg or home recording). • Copyright works included in multimedia projects must give proper attribution to copyright holder.
Music (for integration into multimedia or video projects)	• Records • Cassette tapes • CDs • Audio clips on the Web	• Up to 10 percent of a copyright musical composition may be reproduced, performed, and displayed as part of a multimedia program produced by an educator or students.	• A maximum of 30 seconds per musical composition may be used. • Multimedia program must have an educational purpose.
Computer Software	• Software (purchased) • Software (licensed)	• Library may lend software to patrons. • Software may be installed on multiple machines, and distributed to users via a network. • Software may be installed at home and at school. • Libraries may make copies for archival use or to replace lost, damaged, or stolen copies if software is unavailable at a fair price or in a viable format.	• Only one machine at a time may use the program. • The number of simultaneous users must not exceed the number of licenses; and the number of machines being used must never exceed the number licensed. A network license may be required for multiple users. • Take aggressive action to monitor that copying is not taking place (unless for archival purposes).
Internet	• Internet connections • World Wide Web	• Images may be downloaded for student projects and teacher lessons. • Sound files and video may be downloaded for use in multimedia projects (see portion restrictions above).	• Resources from the Web may not be reposted onto the Internet without permission. However, links to legitimate resources can be posted. • Any resources you download must have been legitimately acquired by the Web site.
Television	• Broadcast (e.g., ABC, NBC, CBS, UPN, PBS, and local stations) • Cable (e.g., CNN, MTV, HBO) • Videotapes made of broadcast and cable TV programs	• Broadcasts or tapes made from broadcast may be used for instruction. • Cable channel programs may be used with permission. Many programs may be retained by teachers for years— see Cable in the Classroom (www.ciconline.org) for details.	• Schools are allowed to retain broadcast tapes for a minimum of 10 school days. (Enlightenedrights holders, such as PBS's ReadingRainbow, allow for much more.) • Cable programs are technically not covered by the same guidelines as broadcast television.

Sources: United States Copyright Office Circular 21;Sections 107,108,and 110 of the Copyright Act (1976) and subsequent amendments, including the Digital Millennium Copyright Act; *Fair Use Guidelines for Educational Multimedia*; cable systems (and their associations); and *Copyright Policy and Guidelines for California's School Districts*, California Department of Education. Note: Representatives of the institutions and associations who helped to draw up many of the above guidelines wrote a letter to Congress dated March 19,1976, stating: "There may be instances in which copying that does not fall within the guidelines stated [above] may nonetheless be permitted under the criterion of fair use."

Source: Use of this material is by permission of the publisher; http://www.halldavidson.net.

GRADING AND ACADEMIC REQUIREMENTS

Courts traditionally have been reluctant to interfere in cases involving academic matters. The prevailing view of the courts is that professional educators are better prepared to render decisions regarding academic issues, particularly those involving student evaluation. Requirements regarding progress from one grade to another typically are not reviewable by the courts unless there is substantial evidence of unreasonableness. For example, the Fourth Circuit Court of Appeals refused to intervene in the failure of a school district to promote to the third grade students who failed to pass a reading level test.[3] The court respected the educational judgment of professional educators, even though the students' intelligence indicated that they were capable of reading at the third-grade level. The students could not be promoted until they demonstrated mastery of the requisite reading skill. One court observed that academic matters by their very nature are more subjective and evaluative than typical issues presented in disciplinary decisions, and such academic judgments should be left to professional educators.[4]

Student Testing

It is well established that the state has the authority to promulgate promotion and graduation requirements. Educators are provided considerable discretion in matters relating to appropriate academic requirements. Often, standardized tests are used to determine student competencies. If the measures are reasonable and nondiscriminatory, they will generally be supported by the courts. Generally, courts are not equipped to evaluate academic performance issues.[5] Thus, the courts limit themselves to addressing issues relating to due process, discriminatory impact, and arbitrary or capricious acts by school personnel. Therefore, the state's authority to develop and assess student performance standards is not debatable.

Grading

The courts have consistently held that educators are highly qualified to assess student progress and assign grades accordingly so long as the standards on which grades are assigned are properly documented, and school and district grading policies are followed. There is no basis for court scrutiny or intervention, as cited in *Owasso Independent School District v. Falvo*.[6] In that case the courts upheld the practice of students' scoring one another's papers as the teacher explained the correct answer to the entire class. Although peer grading was supported in this case, this process should be avoided, since teachers are responsible for evaluating students and for assigning grades.

Grade Reduction for Absences

Excessive student absenteeism poses a challenge for school officials, who often resort to grade reductions as a means to curb this problem. Courts will generally support reasonable policies regarding grade reduction for excessive absences if the policies do not conflict with state statute. School district policy should provide guidance for teachers on this issue.

Grade Reduction for Unexcused Absences

School rules that penalize students academically for unexcused absences, or truancy, are not uncommon. Courts have been more supportive of schools regarding this type of rule than one that mandates grade reduction based on general misconduct. In fact, courts have been quite consistent since the mid-1970s in ruling against school districts for grade reduction related to misconduct. However, school districts must be certain that their rules in the area of truancy are carefully defined. The following case illustrates this point.

In a New Jersey school district, school board policy mandated that a student receive a zero in all subjects on those days he or she was truant from school. The student could make up any tests missed on such days, but the zero had to be used when grades were averaged for the term. In ruling for the student who challenged the rule, the New Jersey Commissioner of Education found the penalty to be excessive.[7] In some instances a student could receive a failing grade in a class for even a single absence. A major reason the school board lost its case appears to be the severity of the penalty rather than the use of grade reduction in general.

Grade Reduction for Academic Misconduct

A number of school districts have formulated policies requiring grade reductions for misconduct. The courts' position regarding such grade reduction is illustrated in the following case.[8]

Two students participated as guitar players in the high school band program. The band director forbade band members to deviate from the planned musical program during band performances, and specifically forbade guitar solos during the performances. In direct defiance of those rules, the two students played two unauthorized guitar pieces at a band program. Consequently, both students received an F for the band course, and that grade prevented one student from graduating with honors. Both students appealed the district court's decision, which favored the school. The court concluded that the school's actions violated no right under federal civil rights statutes.

In yet another case, in Indiana, a student's grade was reduced as punishment for alcohol-related misconduct. The student's parents brought suit against the district, which then moved for summary judgment. The district court held that a high school rule mandating a 4% reduction in grades for each day a student was suspended for alcohol use during school hours was invalid and a violation of substantive due process. The court stated further that the policy was arbitrary, and the school failed to demonstrate a reasonable relationship between the use of alcohol during school hours and a reduction in grades.[9] In an earlier case, the New Jersey Commissioner had ruled that the use of grades as punishment is usually ineffective in producing the desired results and is educationally indefensible. "Whatever system of grades a school may devise will have serious limitations at best, and it must not be further limited by attempting to serve disciplinary purposes also."[10]

Physical Punishment for Poor Academic Performance

Physical punishment of public school students for failure to maintain acceptable academic standards has not received support by the courts. Courts have consistently ruled against teachers' and school officials' use of physical punishment when the student's behavior did not involve improper conduct. For example, one court ruled against physical punishment of a student who failed to perform at an athletically desired level, even though the coach considered the punishment to be instructive and a source of encouragement to the student.[11] U.S. courts have consistently held that public school students should not be physically punished for conduct not related to disciplinary infractions. Furthermore, students should not be physically punished for failure to complete homework or other assignments. School officials may adopt policies calling for academic penalties such as a loss of credit for failure to meet academic assignments, but under no circumstances should physical punishment be inflicted in cases involving academic matters. Corporal punishment for nonacademic misbehavior by students continues to be supported by the courts; however, its use can lead to allegations of cruel and excessive punishment and should be avoided if possible.

GUIDES

Grading and Academic Requirements

1. Competency tests are supported by the courts when there is no evidence of discriminatory intent.
2. Lowering of academic grades as a punitive measure for misbehavior is illegal and indefensible.
3. Students may be penalized academically for unexcused absences or truancy if state statute permits. However, policies in this area should be carefully drawn to ensure fairness.
4. Physical punishment for poor performance has not been supported by the courts. Corporal punishment, when used, must be associated with improper conduct.

EDUCATIONAL MALPRACTICE

Over the last three decades, lawsuits on the grounds of educational malpractice have emerged as a formidable threat to educators. Parents are increasingly bringing suits on behalf of their children, alleging that teachers were either negligent or incapable of providing competent instruction or of properly placing or classifying their children. In these cases, students have charged that they suffered academic injury by being denied the full benefits of a proper education.

Although numerous suits have been filed, to date no case has been won by parents or students. However, with the emergence of school-based management, national teaching standards, the NCLB Act, greater teacher accountability, and emphasis on professionalism in education, the prospect of a successful malpractice challenge may be greatly heightened.

Educational malpractice generally is considered to be any unprofessional conduct or lack of sufficient skill in the performance of professional duties by an educator. It represents a different type of injury to students: an injury that is not physical—but emotional, psychological, or educational—and that results from poor teaching, improper placement, or inappropriate testing procedures.

Because the courts have prescribed duties for teachers to instruct, supervise, and provide for the safety of children, a breach of these duties resulting in injury to students may form adequate grounds for a liability suit. Teacher liability, however, may differ from state to state.

In cases involving alleged academic injury to students, courts have faced the very difficult task of determining exactly where actual fault lies. First, does the alleged injury rest with the student's inability to acquire basic or minimal skills owing to the student's lack of competency or motivation? Second, does the alleged injury rest with the teacher's inability to meet minimal standards of teaching? Further, if teachers are determined to be at fault, is it a single teacher, a select few, or all teachers involved in a child's educational experiences? Because of these difficult questions, courts have failed to support charges of malpractice. Also, because teachers historically have had no direct influence over school policies, curriculum, working conditions, or resource acquisition, they could not reasonably be held to a strict standard of liability. However, with the emergence of teacher empowerment, school-based management, and national teaching and certification standards, the courts may be better able to determine whether malpractice has occurred and precisely where it has occurred. Teachers should be certain to teach and reteach skills when students initially fail to master the required skills. Teachers should also document skills that have been taught and retaught. Documented remediations are important components of the teaching and learning processes.

GUIDES

Educational Malpractice

1. School districts should develop quality standards of practice as a means to guide the instructional program within schools.
2. Teachers should be certain that they are well prepared and highly focused on their instructional duties.
3. Teachers should ensure that all required competencies and skills are taught in the classroom.
4. School districts should provide remediation for students who fail to master required skills and competencies or for those who have difficulty learning.

5. School districts should make informed decisions regarding the appropriateness of curriculum, textbooks, and instructional policies.
6. Teachers should develop flexible and varied instructional strategies and techniques to meet individual needs of students.
7. School districts should use well-prepared promotion and retention standards as guides to decisions affecting student progress.
8. Teachers should be certain that curricula objectives are translated into topics actually taught in the classroom.
9. School districts should avoid inappropriate testing procedures that could result in misclassification or inappropriate placement of students.
10. School districts should develop proper means to monitor instructional practices to improve the overall education delivery system.

PRACTICAL TIPS

Do:

1. Follow prescribed curriculum policy guides in your classroom. Repeated failure to do so can result in charges of insubordination.
2. Understand and meet performance expectations prescribed by your school district under NCLB accountability standards. Meeting performance expectations will generate positive teacher evaluations, and student achievement will likely be enhanced.
3. Make certain that fair use measures are not abused when copyrighted materials are used in your classroom. Failure to do so may result in legal challenges by the authors of copyrighted documents.
4. Understand that your personal records on school-owned computers are not private records. Computers should be used for school business only, unless policy permits exceptions.
5. Make certain that students' grades are assigned in a manner that can be properly documented and defended if necessary. Lack of proper documentation invites challenges by parents and students alike.

Do not:

1. Use grades to penalize a student for behavioral infractions not related to academic performance. Courts

will not support the misapplication of grades for non-academic purposes.

2. Punish a child physically for inability to meet academic expectations. Physical punishment, if permitted, must adhere to school and district policy and address issues related to student behavior and conduct.

3. Use tests to isolate low-performing students when such isolation results in gender or racial disparities. The Fourteenth Amendment may be used to challenge this practice. Such a practice may also affect the self-esteem of low-performing students.

4. Assign grades without documentation demonstrating that skills have been taught and retaught to students who have experienced difficulty achieving prescribed learning outcomes. Student learning outcomes are increasingly being linked to teacher effectiveness.

5. Invite a malpractice lawsuit for failure to provide competent instruction or proper classification of students on the basis of indefensible documentation. Parents are more inclined to file lawsuits in cases of student academic failure in the absence of well-documented academic and instructional records.

ENDNOTES

1. *Warner Jackson et al. v. Superintendent of Public Instruction,* 213 Wis. 2d 1, 570 N.W.2d 407 (1998).
2. Ibid.
3. *Sandlin v. Johnson,* 643 F.2d 1027 (4th Cir. 1981).
4. *Board of Curators of the University of Missouri v. Horowitz,* 435 U.S. 78, 985 S. Ct. 948 (1978).
5. Ibid.
6. *Owasso Independent School District No. I-011 v. Falvo,* 534 U.S. 426; 122 S. Ct. 934; 151 L. Ed. 2d 896 (2002).
7. *Minorities v. Board of Education of Phillipsburg,* N.J. Commissioner of Ed. (1972).
8. *Dunn and McCollough v. Fairfield Community High School District No. 225,* 158 F.3d 962; U.S. App. (1998).
9. *Smith v. School City of Hobart et al. Defendants,* 811 F. Supp. 391, 80 Ed. Law Rept. 839 (Ind. 1993).
10. *Wermuth v. Bernstein and Board of Education of the Township of Livingston* (Dec. N.J. Comm. Ed, 1965).
11. *Hogenson v. Williams,* 542 S.W. 2d 256 (TX App. 1976).

3

Religion and Public Schools

PRAYER, BIBLE READING, AND RELIGIOUS SYMBOLS

The tension that exists today over church–state issues relates to the requirement that the government maintain a neutral position toward religion. In 1879 the U.S. Supreme Court, in the landmark case *Reynolds v. United States*, invoked Thomas Jefferson's view that there should be a wall of separation between church and state.[1]

The First Amendment to the U.S. Constitution serves as the basis for delineating certain individual religious rights and freedoms, as well as governmental prohibitions regarding religion. The First Amendment states, "Congress shall make no laws respecting an establishment of religion or prohibiting the free exercise thereof; or abridging the freedom of speech, or of the press; or of the right of the people peaceably to assemble and to petition the government for a redress of grievances."

Although the intent of the First Amendment was to prohibit Congress from making laws establishing a religion or forbidding individuals to exercise their religious rights, the U.S. Supreme Court, in a compelling 1940 decision, *Cantwell v. Connecticut*, held that this prohibition directed toward Congress applied to the states as well.[2] The Fourteenth Amendment made the First Amendment applicable to state actions, thus providing the same constitutional guarantees to citizens against state infringement on their religious rights by prohibiting the establishment of religious practices in public schools.

The First Amendment contains two essential clauses regarding religion: the *Establishment Clause* and the *Free Exercise Clause*. The establishment clause prohibits the state from passing laws respecting an establishment of religion, aiding a religion, or showing preference for one religion over another.

The free exercise clause prohibits the state from interfering with individual religious freedoms. It protects the right of citizens to choose any religious belief and engage in religious practices.

The combined effect of these two clauses requires that public schools, as state agencies, maintain a neutral position regarding religious matters. This means that the state can neither aid nor inhibit religion—it must adhere to the principle of neutrality. Since the *Cantwell* decision, which held that the Fourteenth Amendment makes the First Amendment applicable to state actions, the establishment clause has held significant legal implications for the administration of public schools.

The establishment clause affects school personnel when they act as state agents. When school personnel are not acting in this capacity, the establishment clause does not restrict their individual religious freedom. Freedom of religion is protected for school personnel, just as it is for other citizens.

School-Sponsored Prayer

The issue of prayer in public schools was addressed by the U.S. Supreme Court in the early 1960s in the landmark *Engel v. Vitale* case. Prior to this time, prayer was routinely offered in public schools across the nation and generally supported by the courts. In 1962 the New York State Board of Regents required the reading of a school-sponsored, nondenominational, voluntary prayer that was to be recited by each class in the presence of the classroom teacher. This prayer was composed by the New York State Board of Regents.

Those students who did not wish to recite the prayer were excused from participation. The requirement that the prayer be recited was challenged by parents on the grounds that it violated the establishment clause of the First Amendment and was in conflict with the beliefs and religious orientation of some students. The court held for the parents in ruling that the prayer was religious in nature and presenting it for recitation by the class did in fact violate the establishment clause of the First Amendment and was illegal This ruling has been consistently reinforced by numerous court decisions since 1962.

In spite of the landmark decision, the inclusion of school prayer continues to be challenged by Congress, state legislatures, and citizens as they persist in seeking creative ways to support prayer in public schools.[3] It remains a highly contested issue as persistent lawmakers in many states continue their efforts to reinstate some form of government-sanctioned prayer in public schools.

Consequently, school prayer remains at the center of controversy in public schools. The courts have been consistent in holding that prayer sanctioned by public schools is a violation of the establishment clause of the First Amendment. Therefore, school personnel must remain neutral in matters involving prayer in public schools. However, the courts also have been somewhat consistent in holding that private devotional activities initiated by students, with no involvement or encouragement by school personnel, and that do not disrupt school activities, are permissible. Whether prayer in public school is permissible largely depends on who schedules it.

Silent Prayer and Meditation

In recent years, some state legislatures have attempted to support some form of state-sponsored voluntary prayer or meditation in public schools. Their efforts, however, have largely been unsuccessful. Numerous challenges to these types of statutes or practices have been led by opposing parents and citizens. Their challenges cover a full range of school activities, such as meditation and prayer at school-sponsored athletic events and graduation ceremonies, both of which will be discussed later in this chapter.

The U.S. Supreme Court responded to the matter of silent meditation and prayer by ruling, in the 1985 *Wallace v. Jaffree* case, that a period of silence set aside for meditation or voluntary prayer in the public school is in violation of the First Amendment.[4] Therefore, teachers must refrain from endorsing any school-sanctioned silent prayer and meditation activities.

Prayer at School Events

In the 1960s and 1970s, courts were less inclined to rule against the use of prayer at baccalaureate and graduation services. These activities were viewed as traditional and ceremonial and, in many cases, consistent with community sentiments. However, in the mid-1980s, lower courts began to rule against prayer at these ceremonies, holding that the use of prayer violated the establishment clause. In a leading 1992 Rhode Island case, *Lee v. Weisman*,[5] the court invalidated the school district's policy that allowed clergy to be invited to deliver invocations and benedictions at middle and high school graduation ceremonies. The clergy's participation was held to be a violation of the establishment clause. The court further noted that, in some instances, students were required to attend these ceremonies, with the possibility that peer pressure would influence them to participate. The court was not convinced that voluntary attendance lessened the impact of the constitutional violation.

The court's ban on prayer at graduation ceremonies led school officials to seek more creative methods to include prayer in these ceremonies. For example, in a significant development, the U.S. Supreme Court upheld a stunning appeals court decision permitting student-initiated, student-led prayer at the Clear Creek Independent School District's graduation ceremonies in Texas. In this 1992 decision, *Jones v. Clear Creek*, a federal appeals court ruled that a Texas school district's policy of allowing each high school senior class to decide whether to offer student-initiated and student-led prayers at its graduation ceremony does not violate the First Amendment ban on the government's establishment of religion. The factors that influenced the court's ruling were as follows:

1. The prayer was initiated by students.
2. School personnel played no role and were not involved in any aspects of the decision.
3. The school had no policy calling for student-initiated prayer at graduation ceremonies but, rather, offered an opportunity for students to make a 2-minute speech at the beginning and end of the ceremony.
4. The student's speech was not censored.
5. Students possess First Amendment rights to free expression.

In a contrasting case, the U.S. Supreme Court in 2000 invalidated student-led prayer at graduation and other school events in *Santa Fe Independent School Dist. v. Doe.*[6] In this case, there was evidence that the school supported, by school policy, the delivery of prayer over the public address system by the student council chaplain at each home game. The U.S. Court of Appeals for the Fifth Circuit had held that the policy was invalid because it violated the establishment clause of the First Amendment and decided that "the words 'nonsectarian, nonproselytizing' are constitutionally necessary components" of a policy governing prayer. Moreover, it also decided that these student-led prayers were acceptable only at graduation, not during football games."

In conclusion, the courts have permitted student-initiated prayer involving no school personnel in *Jones v. Clear Creek*[7] in Texas, as well as a 2-minute opening and closing remark delivered by student volunteers of graduating classes in *Adler v. Duval County School Board*[8] in Florida in 1994. Allowing each high school senior class to decide whether to offer a student-initiated and student-led prayer at its graduation did not in these cases violate the First Amendment ban on the government's establishment of religion. The facts revealed that each district's policy upheld a secular purpose of safeguarding the free speech rights of participating students. The lower courts will usually rely on criteria derived from the 1971 landmark case *Lemon v. Kurtzman,* even though it involved aid to parochial schools. This test is often relied on by lower courts to determine the legality of a practice involving religion in public schools. The *Lemon* standard asserts that a law, policy, or practice must meet the following criteria to be legally valid regarding religion:

1. It must have a secular purpose.
2. It must neither advance, prohibit, nor inhibit religion.
3. It must not create excessive entanglement.[9]

The courts in recent years have abandoned community sentiment in favor of constitutionality. The U.S. Supreme Court's position in *Jones v. Clear Creek* and *Adler v. Duval,* however, may provide an opportunity for some communities to decide whether they wish to have students assume the decision-making role.

School-Sponsored Bible Reading

In 1963, the U.S. Supreme Court addressed the constitutionality of the practice of Bible reading in public schools. Two similar cases reached the court during the same time period. *Abington School District v. Schempp* involved a challenge to the legal validity of a Pennsylvania state statute that required the reading of 10 verses of the Bible, without comment, at the opening of each school day. A companion case, *Murray v. Curlett,* challenged the actual practice of daily Bible reading in Maryland schools.[10]

The U.S. Supreme Court invoked the *primary effect* test to determine the impact of the statute and practice relating to each case. The primary effect test raises the question of whether the primary purpose of a law or practice has the effect of advancing or inhibiting religion and creating excessive entanglement between church and state. If the response to these questions is affirmative, the principle of neutrality has been breached and the action is considered to be an impermissible establishment of religion and a violation of the First Amendment. The court did, however, indicate in *Schempp* that the use of the Bible as a historical, literary, ethics, or philosophical document is permissible if a secular purpose is clearly served. Therefore, teachers may use the Bible as a teaching tool if it is used as a literary or historical document. So long as the Bible serves a secular purpose and is related to the subject taught by a teacher, its use is permissible by the courts.

Religious Symbols

Public schools may not display religious exhibits such as paintings, statutes, pictures, or other visual materials. It may be appropriate, however, for public school teachers to acknowledge and explain the various holidays of all cultural and religious groups as a unit in cultural heritage or some other related subject, as long as a secular purpose is served.

Public school teachers should refrain from the use of religious symbols or pictures, even in conjunction with discussing the various holidays. A case could be made that the presence of the crucifix creates a religious atmosphere in the classroom. The presence of any type of religious symbol or picture would violate the principle of neutrality by creating a devotional atmosphere.

Religious Displays

Religious displays are prohibited in public schools unless they serve a secular purpose. For example, a New Jersey school board policy called for sensitivity to different religions in a manner consistent with the U.S. Constitution. The objective was to teach about religion and its role in the social and historical development of civilization. The policy required the maintenance of calendars in classrooms and in one central location that displayed cultural, ethnic, and religious customs and traditions of various cultures for no more than 10 days during the appropriate season. A group of parents and taxpayers filed a lawsuit against the school board in district court, claiming violations of the First and Fourteenth Amendments to the U.S. Constitution.

In its ruling, the court considered factors such as the age of the children involved, the context in which the government practice appeared, the permanence of the display, whether the symbol was displayed actively or passively, whether the religious holiday has assumed a secular meaning, whether the government practice endorses a particular religion, and whether it is hostile toward religion. The court found that the school board's policy had a secular purpose that did not impermissibly promote religion and did not entangle the government in church–state relationships. Because of the policy's emphasis on religious diversity, it did not favor any particular religion or favor religion over non-religion. The use of religious symbols had a genuine secular purpose that emphasized both tolerance and diversity.[11]

With respect to displays, it is also permissible to employ seasonal decorations such as Santa Claus, reindeer, snow, pine trees, wreaths, eggs, or bunny rabbits. These are considered mere reflections of the joy and merriment associated with various holidays, so long as they are not used to meet a religious purpose.

Consequently, public schools may not erect any type of religious display on school property, such as the nativity scene or the crucifix. However, in 1963, one such display was held by a district court in New York to be a mere passive accommodation of religion.[12] This court supported the erection of a nativity scene on school grounds. The courts today would likely not support such a finding. The presence of a nativity scene on school property would in all probability be interpreted to violate the establishment clause.

Ten Commandments

Two early court decisions, one at the federal district level and the other by the U.S. Supreme Court, held that posting the Ten Commandments in a public school is unconstitutional. North Dakota passed a law requiring the display of a placard that contained the Ten Commandments of the Christian and Jewish religions. The statute called for this display to be located in a conspicuous place in every classroom in public schools. The district court ruled that this practice violated the establishment clause of the First Amendment.[13] Interestingly, in 1980 the Kentucky Supreme Court in *Stone v. Graham*[14] reached a tie decision regarding a statute that required posting the Ten Commandments in public school classrooms. The tie proved to be insignificant, because the U.S. Supreme Court, in a 5–4 decision, held that the statute was unconstitutional and a violation of the establishment clause of the First Amendment.

Prayer at School Board Meetings

School boards that open their meetings with prayer are violating the Constitution's First Amendment establishment clause, according to the U.S. Court of Appeals for the Sixth Circuit, which relied on a series of prayer cases in rendering its decision. A school board initiated a practice of inviting clergy to offer prayer at its meetings, which was challenged by a student and a teacher who frequently attended board meetings. The federal district court upheld the board's practice, finding that the meetings resembled legislative sessions rather than school events, relying on the 1983 U.S. Supreme Court ruling that allowed official prayers at the beginning of state legislative sessions. The student and teacher appealed to the Sixth Circuit court, which noted in its decision that board meetings were held on school property, were regularly attended by students, and did not resemble legislative sessions. The court further emphasized that board meetings had a function that was uniquely directed toward students and school matters, making it necessary for students to attend such meetings on many occasions. The Sixth Circuit court stated that prayer at school board meetings was potentially coercive to students in attendance. The circuit court reversed the district court's ruling, holding that prayer has the tendency to endorse Christianity while excessively entangling the board in religious matters.[15]

GUIDES

Prayer and Bible Use in School

1. Legally defensible guidelines should be developed on the basis of the U.S. Supreme Court decision addressing student-initiated prayer at athletic contests and other school events.
2. School personnel should not be influenced by customs and community expectations to encourage student-initiated prayer at school events.
3. Voluntary student-initiated prayer may be permissible at school events when not endorsed by school personnel.
4. School officials should respond judiciously if alerted that school personnel are encouraging students to offer voluntary prayer at school-sponsored events.
5. School-endorsed prayer in public school violates the establishment clause of the First Amendment and should be avoided if not completely student initiated.
6. Prayer at school board meetings violates the establishment clause, creates excessive entanglement, and cannot be justified on the basis that such meetings are similar to legislative sessions.
7. Teachers may use the Bible for secular purposes in conjunction with a history, literature, or related class. The use of the Bible as a religious document violates the establishment clause of the First Amendment.

RELIGIOUS ACTIVITIES AND HOLIDAY PROGRAMS

The observance of holidays by public schools is clearly an unconstitutional activity if conducted in a devotional atmosphere. The First Amendment prohibits states from either aiding religion or showing preference for one religion over another. Public schools may not celebrate religious holidays. No worship or devotional services, or religious pageants or plays of any nature, should be held in the school. However, certain programs may be conducted if a secular purpose is clearly served.

For example, the district court upheld the school's Christmas program in South Dakota when certain parents challenged the religious content of a Christmas program that was sponsored based on school district policy. The district's policy was challenged on the grounds that it violated the establishment clause of the First Amendment. The U.S. District Court of South Dakota held for the school district in ruling that the performance of music containing religious content does not inherently constitute a religious activity, as long as it serves an educational rather than a religious purpose.[16]

Schools, however, are prohibited from the use of sacred music that occurs in a devotional setting. This type of music may be sung or played as a part of a music appreciation class, so long as a secular purpose is served. School choirs and assemblies may be permitted to sing or play holiday carols, so long as these activities are held for entertainment purposes rather than religious purposes.

Distribution of Religious Materials

Public school personnel are not permitted to distribute religious materials, such as pamphlets or religious literature, on school premises. This practice is a clear violation of the establishment clause. The courts are split regarding whether public school officials may allow religious groups to distribute religious materials on school grounds. Two cases illustrate the courts' posture regarding the distribution of religious materials.

One case involving the distribution of religious material arose in Florida when an elementary school student brought religious pamphlets to distribute to her classmates. When the student requested, through her teacher, to be allowed to distribute the pamphlets, they were confiscated and taken to the principal, who subsequently destroyed them, indicating that he could not permit the distribution of religious material at school.

The student and her mother filed a suit in the U.S. District Court, seeking a preliminary injunction against enforcement of the policy that prohibited the distribution of religious material on school premises. The court held that the motion was premature and that the policy had never been applied by the school. The U.S. Court of Appeals for the Eleventh Circuit affirmed the district court's decision. The district court then addressed the student's request for a permanent injunction against enforcing the policy. The court discerned that the policy was a content-based prior restraint ban on free speech that could be justified only with a showing that the literature would materially or substantially disrupt the operations of the school or infringe on the rights of other students.

In the absence of this showing, the school district's policy, as expected, could not be supported under the law. The court held for the student by issuing a permanent injunction against the enforcement of the policy and also awarded nominal damages and attorney fees.[17]

In the other leading case, *Tudor v. Board of Education*,[18] the highest court in New Jersey in 1954 struck down an attempt by The Gideons International to distribute the Gideon Bible throughout the public schools.

In *Rusk v. Crestview Local School District*, the Sixth Circuit court held that a school could distribute third-party flyers so long as students would not be able to participate in the advertised activity without parental permission.[19]

The courts have also held that schools may exercise limited discretion in determining which flyers may be sent home with students. The Ninth Circuit court ruled in *Hills v. Scottsdale Unified School District* that a school may not refuse to distribute literature advertising a program with underlying religious content when it distributed quite similar literature for secular summer programs.[20] Such restrictions constitute viewpoint discrimination. School officials may, however, refuse to distribute literature that contains proselytizing language.

Pledge of Allegiance

Landmark Case

A 2002 landmark case, *Newdow v. United States*, challenging the daily ritual of reciting the Pledge of Allegiance, emerged in the Ninth Circuit court in California regarding the constitutionality of the inclusion of the phrase "under God." The outcome of the ruling in this case had a profound effect on public schools, on state and federal governments, as well as on U.S. citizens in general. Forty-nine states filed briefs supporting the Pledge of Allegiance.

The case arose when Michael R. Newdow, an atheist and a noncustodial parent, filed a suit on behalf of his 8-year-old daughter, challenging the inclusion of "under

God" in the pledge. A panel of the U.S. Court of Appeals for the Ninth Circuit in San Francisco created quite a controversy when it ruled 2–1 that the inclusion of "under God" was an unconstitutional establishment of religion by the government.[21]

On June 14, 2004, the U.S. Supreme Court overturned the Ninth Circuit court's decision on technical grounds and preserved the contested phrase "one nation under God" in the Pledge of Allegiance. The Supreme Court ruled that Newdow, the plaintiff, had no legal standing to challenge the pledge, because he was not the custodial parent of his now-10-year-old daughter and could not legally represent her. However, this ruling failed to address whether the inclusion of the reference to God was an impermissible practice involving an unconstitutional blending of church and state. Consequently, the U.S. Supreme Court's ruling does not prevent a future lawsuit challenging the inclusion of the phrase "one nation under God" in the pledge. In fact, Newdow and three other plaintiffs later filed another challenge. Interestingly, in 1943 the U.S. Supreme Court in *West Virginia State Board of Education v. Barnette* held that public school officials shall not require students to salute and pledge allegiance to the flag.[22] These activities must be strictly voluntary.

GUIDES

Religious Activities

1. School-sponsored holiday programs are permitted if they do not create a religious atmosphere and if they have a secular purpose. School districts may find it difficult to justify the posting of the Ten Commandments or other references to God as meeting a purely secular purpose.
2. Religious pageants, displays, or symbols will not meet the constitutional requirements of neutrality by school officials. However, statues or pictures may be used to teach art form if taught as a secular activity.
3. The distribution of religious material by external groups may or may not be permitted, depending on the particular court involved. However, a student may be allowed to distribute religious pamphlets if the distribution does not interfere with normal school activities or create material or substantial disruption.
4. School officials must respect the free exercise of rights by students, unless the exercise of those rights violates the rights of others or disrupts the educational process.

5. Educators must refrain from any activity that would create an unclear line of separation between school activities and religious activities.

6. Students shall not be compelled to recite the Pledge of Allegiance, on the grounds that compelling them to do so would violate their right to freedom of expression.

PRACTICAL TIPS

Do:

1. Make certain that school or district policies regarding religious issues are clearly understood and followed judiciously to avoid legal challenges based on church–state violations.

2. Understand that your students have a First Amendment free exercise right to participate in private student-initiated devotional activities in your school. If private participation does not create disruption, violate school rules, or infringe on the rights of others, it must be permitted.

3. Know the types of classroom bulletin board displays that are permitted during the various holidays. Lack of knowledge can result in a First Amendment violation regarding the establishment of religion in your school.

4. Make certain that student projects involving religious content are not rejected purely on the basis of religious content when other, nonreligious student projects are not treated similarly.

5. Adhere to the establishment clause requirement by not using your classroom to promote religion. The use of the classroom as a religious forum violates First Amendment rights regarding religion.

Do not:

1. Lead or offer prayer in your classroom. Such action constitutes a violation of the establishment clause and of student rights.

2. Initiate discussion on religion unless it is secular and related to an approved curriculum in which you have been assigned to teach, such as a Bible class or a history, philosophy, or comparative literature class.

3. Coerce students to stand and recite the Pledge of Allegiance unless it is prescribed by school or district policy. Students have a right to refuse to do so as long as their refusal does not infringe on the rights of other students who elect to participate.

4. Encourage students to engage, or discourage students from engaging, in religious activities. Teachers must remain neutral in all matters involving religion in their schools.

5. Encourage students who are assigned to speak at graduation ceremonies or other school functions to include religious content in their speech. Courts will not recognize the application of the free exercise clause if the student's religious speech was initiated or encouraged by school personnel.

ENDNOTES

1. *Reynolds v. United States*, 98 U.S. (8 OTTO) 145 (1879).
2. *Cantwell v. Connecticut*, 310 U.S. 296 (1940).
3. *Engel v. Vitale*, 370 U.S. 421, 82 S. Ct. 1261 (1962).
4. *Wallace v. Jaffree*, 472 U.S. 38, 105 S. Ct. 2479 (1985).
5. *Lee v. Weisman*, 505 U.S. 577 (1992).
6. *Santa Fe Independent School District v. Doe*, 120 S. Ct. 2266; 147 L. Ed. 2d 295 (2000).
7. *Jones v. Clear Creek Independent School District*, 977 F.2d 963 (5th Cir. 1992).
8. *Adler v. Duval County School Board*, 851 F. Supp. 446 (M.D. Fla. 1994).
9. *Lemon v. Kurtzman* and *Early v. Dicenso*, 403 U.S. 602, 91 S. Ct. 2105 (1971).
10. *School District of Abington Township v. Schempp; Murray v. Curlett*, 374 U.S. 203, 83 S. Ct. 1650 (1965).
11. *Clever v. Cherry Hill Township Board of Education*, 838 F. Supp. 929 (D.N.J. 1993).
12. *Lawrence v. Buchmuller*, 40 Misc. 2d 300, 243 N.Y.S. 2d 87, 91 (Sup. Ct. 1963).
13. *Ring v. Grand Forks School District No. 1*, 483 F. Supp. 272 (N.D. 1980).
14. *Stone v. Graham*, 599 S.W.2d. 157 (Ky. 1980).
15. *Coles v. Cleveland Board of Education*, 1999, WL 144262 (6th Cir. 1999).
16. *Florey v. Sioux Falls School District*, 464 F. Supp. 911 (D.S.D. 1979).
17. *Johnson-Loehner v. O'Brien*, 859 F. Supp. 575 (M.D. Fla. 1994).
18. *Tudor v. Board of Education of Borough of Rutherford*, 14 N.J. 31, 100 A.2d 857 (1953), *cert. denied.* 348 U.S. 816, 75 S. Ct. 25, 99 L. Ed. 664 (1954).
19. *Rusk v. Crestview Local School District*, 379 F.3d 418 (2004).
20. *Hills v. Scottsdale Unified School District*, 329 F.3d 1044 (2003).
21. *Newdow v. United States*, 315 F.3d 497 (C.A. 9, 2002).
22. *West Virginia State Board of Education v. Barnette*, 319 U.S. 624, 63 S. Ct. 1178 (1943).

4

Students, the Law, and Public Schools

School officials are granted broad powers to establish rules and regulations governing student conduct in public schools. These powers, however, are not absolute. They are subject to the standard of reasonableness. Generally, rules are deemed to be reasonable if they are necessary to maintain an orderly and peaceful school environment and advance the education process. The courts, in determining the enforceability of policies, rules, and regulations, require evidence of sufficient justification by school officials of the need to enforce the policy, rule, or regulation. Because students enjoy many of the same constitutional rights as adults, courts have been very diligent in ensuring that their constitutional rights be protected.

Although school rules are necessary to ensure proper order and decorum, they should not be so broad or nebulous as to allow for arbitrary and inconsistent interpretation. Fundamental fairness requires that students understand what behavior is required of them by school personnel. Rules should be sufficiently definite in providing students with adequate information regarding expected behavior.

Further, in determining whether policies or regulations are fair and reasonable, it is necessary to assess them in the context of their application. Whether a rule or regulation is legally defensible depends on the facts in the situation.

The concept of *in loco parentis* (in place of parent) has permitted educators to promulgate rules that allow them to exercise a reasonable degree of control over students under their supervision. This concept, however, is not without limits. School officials and teachers do not fully occupy the place of the parent. Their control or jurisdiction is limited

to school functions and activities. Although in loco parentis is considered a viable concept, it requires prudence on
the part of school officials and teachers. Prudence in this
instance implies that educators' actions must be consistent with those of the average parent under the same or
similar circumstances. Whereas children are subject to
reasonable rules and regulations promulgated by school
officials, they enjoy personal rights that must be recognized and respected. However, in loco parentis does allow
teachers to control student conduct in the classroom, so
long as their actions are reasonable and fair regarding the
treatment of students.

FREEDOM OF EXPRESSION

Freedom of expression is derived from the First Amendment to the U.S. Constitution, which provides, in part, that
"Congress shall make no law . . . abridging the freedom of
speech, or of the press; or the right of the people peaceably
to assemble."

Stated differently, the First Amendment to the Constitution guarantees the right to freedom of speech to U.S.
citizens, including students in public schools. This freedom,
however, does not include a license to exercise such rights in
a manner that materially or substantially disrupts the education process. These were the criteria applied by the U.S.
Supreme Court in determining whether regulations prohibiting student expression were constitutionally valid.

The *Tinker* Case

In 1969, the *Tinker* case emerged as a leading case involving student rights. This case arose when three students
wore black armbands to class in protest of the government's policy in Vietnam. They were suspended from
school without any evidence that their protest created
disruption in school. Interestingly, school officials did not
prohibit the wearing of other symbols with political or controversial messages. The students sought a court order to
prevent school officials from disciplining them for exercising their First Amendment rights. The U.S. Supreme Court
held for the students, stating that it was unconstitutional to
discipline students for the peaceful wearing of armbands or
other symbols bearing expressions of opinion unless there
was evidence of material or substantial disruption to the
education process.

In this landmark case, the U.S. Supreme Court for the very first time held that students possess the same constitutional rights as adults and that these rights do not end at the schoolhouse door.[1] This ruling by the High Court significantly altered the relationship between school personnel and students. The *Tinker* ruling clearly mandated that professional educators respect the civil rights of students in public schools. When student rights are restricted, school personnel must demonstrate a justifiable or legitimate reason for the restriction. For example, educators may restrict the rights of a student if they are able to demonstrate that such restriction is necessary to maintain order and proper decorum in the school. A student's rights also may be restricted if the exercise of those rights infringes on the rights of others.

To gain a clearer view of the nature of the litigation involving freedom of expression in the *Tinker* case, consider a contrasting case in the U.S. Court of Appeals for the Fifth Circuit, *Blackwell v. Issaquena County Board of Education*, which emerged in Mississippi when a principal banned the wearing of "freedom" buttons in response to a disturbance caused by students talking noisily in the corridor when they were scheduled to be in class. Students wearing the buttons, which depicted a black and a white hand joined together with "SNCC" inscribed on them, were found pinning them on other students, who objected. Class instruction deteriorated into a state of general confusion and a breakdown in discipline. Students were warned during an assembly program not to wear the buttons. This warning was repeated on the following day. Violators were subsequently suspended. As the suspended students left campus, they attempted to influence other nonviolators to leave with them. The court held for the board of education, upholding the principal's action as reasonable on the basis of factual circumstances surrounding the incidents. The Fifth Circuit justices reasoned that it is always within the province of school authorities to provide by regulation for the prohibition and punishment of acts calculated to undermine the school's routine. "This is not only proper in our opinion, but it is necessary."[2]

In a related case, a student who delivered a lewd speech at a high school assembly while nominating a friend for a student office was suspended for 3 days for using profane language. The U.S. Supreme Court held for the district, stating that the First Amendment does not prevent school officials from disciplining students for indecent speech and protecting other students from vulgar and offensive language.[3] In short, no rights are absolute but, rather, are subject to reasonable restrictions, which must be justified by school personnel.

VIEWPOINT DISCRIMINATION

First Amendment freedom of expression rights are held in high regard by the courts. Consequently, they are judicious in ensuring that these rights are protected. Students and school personal enjoy rights to freedom of expression within reasonable limits, since public schools provide a limited open forum where such rights must be recognized. Although school leaders may restrict expression rights that create material and substantial disruption, demonstrate disrespect for authority, violate school rules, or infringe on the rights of others, officials cannot, however, restrict speech based merely on the content of the expression unless it falls into the preceding categories. Viewpoint discrimination simply means that school leaders may not exhibit prejudice toward a particular viewpoint or silence speech with which they disagree. They may place restrictions based on content but not on viewpoint.

GUIDES

Freedom of Expression

1. School officials may restrict freedom of expression when there is evidence of material and substantial disruption, violation of school rules, destruction of school property, or disregard for authority. In each case, students must be provided minimal due process before any punitive action is taken.
2. Buttons, pamphlets, and other insignia may be banned if the message communicated is vulgar or obscene or mocks others on the basis of race, origin, color, gender, or religion. They may also be banned if their content is inconsistent with the basic mission of the school. School policies that address these issues should be developed and communicated to students and parents.
3. Prohibition of a particular form of expression requires more than a mere desire to avoid the discomfort and unpleasantness associated with an unpopular view. Such action is arbitrary, capricious, and indefensible.
4. Speech content may be regulated under certain conditions but not the views expressed by the speech.

PROTESTS AND DEMONSTRATIONS

Protests and demonstrations are considered forms of free expression. Therefore, students are afforded the right to participate in these activities under certain conditions. So long as these activities are peaceful, do not violate school rules, and do not result in destruction of school property, protests and demonstrations are allowed. Because school officials are charged with the responsibility to protect the health and safety of all students and to provide an orderly school environment, they may regulate the time, place, and manner of conducting such activities. Such regulations, however, are considered to be mere conditions rather than prohibitions.

School officials should anticipate that minor disruptions such as noise and crowding in corridors may occur when there is disagreement or when opposite points of view are expressed regarding various issues in schools. The courts concur that minor disruptions must be tolerated by school officials. School officials may justifiably restrict students' rights to free speech only when they can demonstrate that a particular form of expression has caused or will likely cause material and substantial disruption.

GUIDES

Protests and Demonstrations

1. Demonstrations that deprive other students of the right to pursue their studies in an orderly and peaceful environment can be disallowed.
2. Students engaged in demonstrations and protests shall not obstruct the corridors or prevent free movement among students who are not participants in these activities.
3. Any activities associated with demonstrations and protests that result in disrespect for authority, destruction of property, violations of school rules, or any other unlawful activities may be banned.
4. An activity involving students' right to freedom of expression shall not be banned because it creates discomfort or conflicts with the views of school officials.
5. The time, place, and manner of the distribution of pamphlets, buttons, and insignia may be regulated by school officials. Prohibiting distribution in class during regular school hours or in the corridors between classes is considered reasonable.
6. Unsubstantiated fear and apprehension of disturbance are not sufficient grounds to restrict the right to freedom of expression.

SCHOOL-SPONSORED NEWSPAPERS

Courts generally hold that a school publication has the respon-sibility for providing a forum for students to express their ideas and views on a variety of topics of interest to the school community. Although the newspaper is intended to repre-sent a forum for student expression, those responsible for its production should be mindful of their obligation to embrace responsible rules of journalism. The school newspaper should reflect editorial policy and sound judgment of student editors, who operate under the guidance of a faculty advisor.

In a leading case in 1987, the U.S. Supreme Court reached a landmark decision in *Hazelwood School District v. Kuhlmeier*. Students in a high school journalism course wrote and edited the school newspaper. The principal reviewed the material prior to publication and deleted two pages containing articles on divorce and teenage pregnancy. The U.S. Supreme Court ruled that public school officials do not violate the First Amendment by exercising editorial con-trol over the content of student speech in school-sponsored newspapers, as long as their actions are reasonably related to valid education purposes.[4]

A newspaper produced as a part of the school's curricu-lum may not enjoy the same privileges as one produced out-side of the school's curriculum. Although in both cases the paper is intended to serve as a forum for student expression, more latitude is extended to students when the paper is not considered a part of the school's curriculum. For example, in the latter case, greater freedom should be granted to student editors in reporting the news when there is no evidence of disruption or defamation. Also, school officials are less likely to incur legal liability if the school's paper is not considered a part of the curriculum. However, if it is considered part of the curriculum, then school officials must be allowed to exercise reasonable control over newspaper content, because they may become liable for defamation involving libel. A curriculum-based newspaper is one that is integrated into the school's curriculum and typically associated with an aca-demic class such as journalism, and school officials may reg-ulate content that is inconsistent with the basic educational mission of the school. School-funded and student-funded papers are not associated with the curriculum and thus enjoy greater flexibility in reporting news.

Although the U.S. Supreme Court's decision in *Hazelwood* provides greater latitude for administrators, courts gener-ally still accept the notion that a school publication has the responsibility for leading opinions, provoking student dialogue, and providing a forum for a variety of student opinions.

Although faculty advisors are generally assigned the responsibility to monitor material written for the student newspaper, in reality their primary responsibility should involve providing advice with respect to form, style, grammar, and appropriateness of material, recognizing that the final decision for printed material rests with student editors. Consequently, student editors, under the guidance of their advisors, should be free to report the news and to editorialize, but at all times they should adhere to the rules of responsible journalism. A faculty advisor may not be punished, demoted, or dismissed for allowing constitutionally protected material to be printed that may prove distasteful to school officials. When justified, school leaders may exercise limited review of school-financed publications so long as they spell out in policy the reason for the review, the time frame involved, the person(s) responsible for reviewing the material, and specifically what material will be reviewed. Students are afforded the right to express their views and ideas that do not materially and substantially affect the operation of the school. Broad censorship by school officials is not permitted and is in violation of the free speech rights of students. In light of these precautions, however, students' free speech rights are not without limits. Material that is libelous, vulgar, or obscene or that mocks others on the basis of race, origin, sex, color, or religion is impermissible.

GUIDES

Student Newspapers

1. With the involvement of representative students, teachers, and community citizens, legally defensible policies should be formulated that govern publication of the school's newspaper.
2. Student editors should be chosen who will exercise high standards of responsible journalism.
3. Administrative prerogatives vary, depending on whether the student newspaper is considered to be a limited open forum or a curriculum-based publication.
4. Student editors have the primary responsibility to see that the newspaper is free of libelous statements and obscenity. Additionally, editors should be reminded that newspapers are subject to the law of libel.

5. Regulations should be developed that prescribe procedures to be followed in the event that prior review is warranted. These should include
   a. a definite period in which the review of materials will be completed,
   b. the specific person to whom the materials will be submitted, and
   c. what specific materials are included for review.

CENSORSHIP

Limited review of school-sponsored publications may be permitted, but broad censorship is not. School officials' commitment to sponsor a student publication should reflect a commitment to respect personal rights associated with freedom of expression. School officials have the option to decide whether they wish to finance a school-sponsored publication. Once a decision is made to support a limited open forum for student ideas, broad censorship powers may not be imposed. School officials must be mindful that students are afforded the right to express their ideas and criticisms when these expressions do not materially and substantially interfere with proper decorum in the school, irrespective of whether the newspaper is considered a part of the school's curriculum or is student sponsored.

GUIDES

Censorship

1. Courts are in disagreement regarding the extent to which school officials may examine and make judgments on student publications prior to their distribution.
2. If prior restraint is invoked, there should be a demonstrated and compelling justification for it.
3. School officials must be able to demonstrate that the distribution of a student publication will create a material and substantial disruption before they make such a charge.
4. If limited review is legally justified, the following safeguards should be included in the review process:
   a. a short deadline for the completion of the review,
   b. an identification of the person(s) vested with the authority to approve or disapprove the material,
   c. the form in which the material is to be submitted,

    d. a clear and specific explanation of the types of items that are prohibited, with a rationale as to why they are prohibited, and

    e. an opportunity and a defined process for students to appeal the decision if they feel that it is unjust.

DRESS AND APPEARANCE

The prevailing view is that issues involving dress should be left to the decisions of state courts, as the U.S. Supreme Court has consistently declined to address this issue. Student dress as a form of free expression is not considered as significant as most other forms of free expression. There is, however, a First Amendment freedom associated with it.

Dress may be regulated if there is a defensible basis for doing so. However, school regulations that violate students' right by being vague or ambiguous or by failing to demonstrate a connection to disruption will not meet court scrutiny. Dress regulations based on fashion or taste as a sole criterion will not survive court scrutiny. School officials, however, may within reason prescribe rules governing student dress and appearance, with an emphasis on reasonableness. In fact, the courts in some cases are now requiring school officials to demonstrate the reasonableness of their rules even before they elect to decide whether constitutional rights of students are violated.

Dress is generally viewed as a form of self-expression reflecting the student's values, background, culture, and personality. Therefore, restrictions on student dress are justified only where there is evidence of material or substantial disruption to the education process. Justifiable reasons for restricting certain types of dress are that they violate health and safety standards or draw unusual attention to a student's anatomy. Examples of clothing that draws attention to a student's anatomy may include sagging pants that reveal underwear, clothing containing large holes, overly short skirts, low-cut halter tops, strapless tops, low-cut necklines, tops with spaghetti straps, low waistbands that expose the body, and sheer or see-through fabrics. The following restrictions have been upheld by the courts regarding dress and appearance:

1. school regulations necessary to protect the safety of students (e.g., wearing of long hair or jewelry around dangerous equipment in laboratories);
2. school regulations necessary to protect the health of students (e.g., requiring students to keep hair clean and free of parasites);

3. rules prohibiting dress that does not meet standards of the community (e.g., dressing in a manner that calls undue attention to one's body); and
4. prohibition of dress that results in material and substantial disruption to the orderly administration of the school (e.g., wearing T-shirts containing vulgar, lewd, or defamatory language based on race, color, gender, national origin, or religion).

Health and Safety Issues

Schools are vested with broad and implied powers designed to protect the health, safety, and welfare of students, and school officials may promulgate reasonable rules and regulations necessary to address these concerns. Thus, situations involving certain types of dress that pose a threat to the safety and well-being of students may be regulated. For example, if a student is wearing excessively long hair in vocational shop classes or laboratories, and the loose hair poses a threat to the student's safety, school officials may take appropriate steps to regulate hair length. The U.S. Court of Appeals for the Fifth Circuit held that there is no constitutional right to wear one's hair in a public school in the length and styles that suits the wearer.[5] Health and safety concerns regarding hair length are generally supported by the courts. Students may be required to wash long hair for hygienic purposes. For example, if certain types of fungus are associated with dirty, long hair, a student may be required to take appropriate steps to rectify the problem.

Hair and grooming regulations are constitutional as long as they are not arbitrary and if they are designed to advance legitimate concerns for maintaining discipline, avoiding disruption, and fostering respect for authority. Similar measures may be taken to regulate the type of jewelry worn if the jewelry poses a potential threat to students' safety in shop, activity-oriented, or physical education classes.

Controversial Slogans

Slogans worn on T-shirts and caps, as well as other media that are in direct conflict with the school's stated mission, may be regulated. Expressions that violate standards of common decency or depict vulgar, lewd, and otherwise obscene gestures also may be regulated. In instances when disruption does occur or when there is a reasonable expectation that disruption might occur, school officials may take appropriate action to rectify the situation. These actions are particularly relevant when the content of such expressions mocks others on the basis of race, gender, color, religion, language, sexual orientation, or national origin.

Courts have not been altogether consistent in their rulings regarding controversial slogans by students. For example, in *Morse v. Frederick*, school officials were supported by the U.S. Supreme Court for disciplining a student for displaying a banner promoting illegal substances, in violation of the school's policy.[6]

In another case, the U.S. Court of Appeals for the Second Circuit upheld a middle school student's right to wear a T-shirt that depicted President George W. Bush as a chicken with a martini on one wing and a cocaine straw in the other. The student's expression was held to be harsh but was deemed to be protected speech under the First and Fourteenth Amendments to the Constitution.[7]

GUIDES

Dress and Appearance

1. Local school dress codes developed by the school should be approved by board of education policies. Faculty, students, parents, and citizens of the local community should be involved in the formulation of such regulations.
2. Dress codes will be supported by the courts only when there is evidence that they are reasonable.
3. Dress and appearance restrictions based on taste, style, and fashion, rather than health, safety, and order, will not pass court scrutiny.
4. Appearance that does not conform to rudiments of decency may be regulated.
5. Dress that is considered vulgar or that mocks others on the basis of race, gender, religion, color, or national origin may be prohibited.

SEARCH AND SEIZURE

The Fourth Amendment to the U.S. Constitution provides protection of all citizens against unreasonable search and seizure. This amendment provides in part that "the right of people to be secure in their persons, houses, papers, and effects, against unreasonable searches and seizures, shall not be violated, and no warrants shall issue, but upon probable cause."

Because students enjoy many of the same constitutional rights as adults, they are granted protection against unreasonable search and seizure. The major challenge facing school personnel involves delicately balancing the student's individual right to Fourth Amendment protection against the school's duty to provide a safe and secure environment for all students.

To search or not to search a pupil's locker, desk, purse, or automobile on school premises presents a perplexing problem for educators. Basic to this issue is the question of precisely what constitutes a reasonable search. The reasonableness of the search becomes the critical issue in cases in which students claim personal violations on the basis of illegal searches.

Most authorities point to the distinction between searches of a student's person and those that involve lockers and desks. The major distinction, of course, is that lockers and desks are considered to be school property. Consequently, school personnel are provided greater latitude in searching lockers and desks than they are in searching a student's person.

The underlying requirement of the Fourth Amendment is that searches and seizures must be reasonable. What, then, constitutes a reasonable search? A reasonable search is a search that clearly does not violate the constitutional rights of students. What is reasonable will depend on the context within which the search takes place.

Reasonable Suspicion

School officials and teachers need only reasonable suspicion to initiate a search. This standard is less rigorous than the requirement involving probable cause. What exactly constitutes reasonable suspicion? Reasonable suspicion is based on information received from students or teachers that is considered reliable. As long as the informant is known rather than anonymous, and the information provided seems credible, courts will generally find little difficulty in supporting administrative actions based on reasonable grounds.

Consequently, certified school personnel may search if reasonable suspicion is established as the primary basis for the search. The courts have declared that in loco parentis cannot stand alone without reasonable suspicion.

Reasonable suspicion was addressed in the landmark 1985 *New Jersey v. T.L.O.* case, when the U.S. Supreme Court reaffirmed that searches conducted by school officials are indeed subject to standards of the Fourth Amendment; however, a warrant requirement in particular is unsuited to the school environment. According to the High Court, requiring the teacher to obtain a warrant before searching a child suspected of an infraction of school rules would unduly interfere with the maintenance of the swift, informal disciplinary procedures needed in the schools.

A search of a student by a teacher or school official must be both "justified at its inception" and "reasonably related in scope to the circumstances which justified the interference in the first place." Simply stated, school personnel should have reasonable grounds to believe a search of a particular student is necessary to provide proof that the student has violated a particular policy, rule, or law. Further, the scope of the search must be limited to the incident at hand. In other words, a sweep search of all students by a teacher in hope of turning up evidence of contraband or violation of rules would be illegal. There should be individualized suspicion. *Individualized* refers to both the individual student and the individual violation.[8] Therefore, indiscriminate searches by teachers are illegal. These types of searches often occur when something of value is missing in the classroom. A search of all students in hope of locating the missing item is illegal. There has to be specific information that leads the teacher to a particular student or group of students to justify a search of those students.

Student Desks

Student desks are subject to search if the standard of reasonableness is met. Desks should never be searched on the basis of a mere "hunch" but, rather, on reliable information that leads teachers to believe that school rules have been violated or that the health or safety of students is threatened. In all cases, searches should be based on clearly written policies that inform students that desks are subject to search if reasonable suspicion is established. School policies should describe the conditions and circumstances under which desk searches will occur. Again, wider discretion is provided to educators in searches involving school property.

Student Lockers

School personnel must meet the same standard of reasonableness in searching student lockers as previously described regarding the search of student desks. Because student lockers provide privacy for students, there is often a greater tendency to expect students to harbor items in lockers that violate school rules or that involve criminal activity. This view alone does not justify an indiscriminate search. Again, students should be informed that lockers will be searched if reasonable suspicion is established to justify a need to search. If a search of a student's locker becomes necessary, the student and at least one other school official should be present to ensure that proper procedures are followed. The affected student should open the locker in the presence of school officials if feasible. This student may also request the presence of another student if he or she wishes. In no cases, except in extreme emergencies such as a bomb threat, should an indiscriminate search be initiated. Barring an emergency, indiscriminate searches of students' lockers are indefensible and illegal.

Book Bags

Searches involving book bags tend to be extremely complex, owing to the intrusive nature of the search itself. A more extensive and intrusive search will likely require stronger evidence to establish reasonable suspicion. At least one court has stated that "we are also of the view that as the intrusiveness of the search intensifies, the standard of Fourth Amendment reasonableness approaches probable cause, even in the school context."[9]

In the 1994 New Jersey case *Desilets v. Clearview Regional Board of Education*, involving book bag searches of students engaged in a field trip, the Superior Court of New Jersey held that the search of students' hand luggage was justified under the Fourth Amendment, based on a legitimate interest of school administrators and teachers in preventing students from taking contraband on field trips.[10] This decision was supported by evidence that students and parents were informed beforehand that a search would be conducted.

Police should not be involved in intrusive book bag searches unless the probable cause standard is met, meaning that a search warrant must be issued. Probable cause is invoked when it is likely that a crime has been committed. Police are typically involved in searches involving concealed weapons, drugs, and gang-related activities.

Automobiles

School officials may search student automobiles parked on school property if the standards of reasonable suspicion are met. Students and parents should be informed by school or district policy that automobiles are subject to reasonable search if there is a legitimate basis for the search.

If the student's automobile is parked on nonschool property, probable cause must be established, and law enforcement officials are required to present a warrant prior to initiation of the search. Again, parents should be informed of an impending search to allow them the opportunity to initiate any steps they deem necessary in this situation. If illegal items such as drugs or weapons are discovered, they are admissible in a court of law.

Personal Searches

Personal searches are not advisable and are strongly discouraged unless there is overwhelming evidence to justify the need for the search. Even then, there should be a sense of urgency based on a belief that the student has in his or her possession some dangerous item that could pose a serious threat to the health and safety of the student or others in the school. Whether a search of this nature is considered reasonable will depend on the facts surrounding the case. The courts will generally establish this standard on the basis of the facts presented, to determine reasonableness. In doing so, they will attempt to balance the student's privacy rights against the interests of school officials who conducted the search.

Personal searches of an intrusive nature should be avoided except under extremely serious circumstances. The more intrusive the search, the more it triggers the need for probable cause, which necessitates the involvement of law enforcement officials. Students should be protected from intrusive body-cavity searches if at all possible. When facts reveal that a personal search is necessary, every precaution should be taken to conduct the search in a private setting, with persons of the same gender conducting the search. The student should be afforded the greatest amount of protection of privacy as possible under the circumstances. If the search involves removal of the student's garments, the student should be allowed to remove, in privacy, any items of clothing the search warrants. He or she should be provided alternative clothing during the search process.

Extreme caution should be taken to ensure, as much as possible, that the student is not demeaned during this process. Unless there is an extreme sense of urgency, it might be advisable to isolate the student, keep the student under observation, and consult with the student's parents or legal guardian. Under all circumstances, parents should be advised of the type of search conducted, the evidence that gave rise to the need to conduct the search, who was involved in conducting the search, and what was discovered during the search process. Personal searches should be considered searches of *last resort* and should be handled in accordance with school or district policy. They should never be calculated to cause embarrassment or mental distress for the student.

Use of Canines

The deployment of canines by school officials has received mixed reviews by the courts, which are almost evenly divided on this issue. However, with the growing incidence of drugs and violence in schools, the courts may eventually reach consensus regarding this issue.

For example, in a questionable decision the U.S. Court of Appeals for the Seventh Circuit held in *Doe v. Renfrow* that school officials stood in loco parentis and had the right to use dogs to seek out drugs.

Simultaneously, the U.S. Court of Appeals for the Tenth Circuit in *Zamoro v. Pomeroy* held for the school in its use of dogs in exploratory sniffing of lockers. The court noted that the school gave notice at the beginning of the school year that lockers may be periodically inspected and furthermore that lockers were jointly possessed by both students and the school.[11] In a different ruling, the federal district court in *Jones v. Latexo Independent School District* held that the use of dogs was too intrusive in the absence on individual suspicion.[12] A similar decision was rendered in *Powers v. Plumas Unified School District* regarding a random canine search in which students were searched as they left a classroom.[13] The court held that a groundless search of students by dog sniffing was unreasonable under the circumstances.

GUIDES

Search and Seizure

1. A student's freedom from unreasonable search should be carefully balanced against the need for the school to maintain order; to maintain discipline; and to protect the health, safety, and welfare of all students.
2. Factors such as the need for the search; the student's age, history, and record of behavior; the gravity of the problem; and the need for an immediate search should be considered before initiating a search.

3. A school search should be based on reasonable grounds for believing that something contrary to school rules or significantly detrimental to the school and its students will be exposed by the search.

4. The information leading to school searches should be independent of involvement by law enforcement officials. Searches involving law enforcement officials must be for probable cause and accompanied by a search warrant.

5. Although the primary purpose for the search should be to secure evidence of student misconduct for school disciplinary purposes, under certain circumstances criminal evidence may be made available to law enforcement officials.

6. Personal searches should be avoided except when imminent danger exists. Such searches can be justified only in cases of extreme emergency where there is an immediate threat to the health and safety of students and school personnel. In such cases, school authorities should be certain that their actions are fully justified, with convincing information to support this more intrusive search.

7. School personnel should conduct the search in a private setting. At best, a search is a demoralizing experience, and great care should be taken to minimize embarrassment to the student.

8. The magnitude of the offense, the extent of intrusiveness, the nature of the evidence sought, and the background of the student involved should be considered before a search is initiated.

9. A pat-down search of a student, if justified, should be conducted by school personnel of the same gender and with an adult witness of the same gender present, if possible. Personal searches conducted by persons of the opposite sex can be very risky.

10. Arbitrary searches or mass shakedowns cannot be justified as reasonable, and are illegal.

11. Canine searches, if used, must be accompanied by compelling evidence to justify their use.

USE OF CELL PHONES

The use of cell phones by public school students has increased in frequency and popularity in recent years. Students find these devices to be affordable and convenient sources of communication both on and off school premises.

Courts in New York and New Jersey have supported the school's authority to ban the use of cell phones in public schools. Courts will likely support similar prohibitions against their use if there is evidence of disruption to the educational process and no violation of students' First Amendment freedoms.

It is well established that school officials may prohibit any practice that materially or substantially disrupts the education process. School districts may minimize legal challenges when there is evidence that the use of cell phones creates disruption or that they are used for improper purposes. School officials are delegated the authority to maintain a safe and orderly environment to facilitate teaching and learning. Consequently, they may prohibit any practice that affects proper order and decorum, as learning cannot occur in a disruptive environment. When school officials provide evidence that cell phones create a disruptive influence in the school and are abused by students, they will likely succeed in prohibiting student possession of these devices on school premises. This prohibition should not violate students' personal rights.

However, school boards, through district policy, may allow special exceptions for cases in which such devices are needed for medical emergencies involving students with chronic illnesses or in other special circumstances that warrant their use. If the use of cell phones is prohibited by policy, all allowable exceptions should be filed and readily available should school officials need to retrieve them if challenged by parents who may raise questions regarding preferential treatment. In the absence of compelling evidence that cell phones are needed by students, school officials will likely succeed without court intervention as long as they consistently adhere to their own policies and demonstrate no evidence of disparate treatment of students regarding permission to use these devices.

GUIDES

Cell Phones

1. The use of cell phones by students should not be banned unless there is sufficient evidence of disruption or improper use.
2. If cell phones are permitted, specific guidelines should be developed governing the conditions under which they may be used.

3. If cell phones are not permitted for general use, exceptions should be allowed that involve medical emergencies or other special circumstances that warrant the use of these devices.
4. Policies or guidelines should always be driven by a sense of fairness and due consideration for the unique and personal needs of students.

CORPORAL PUNISHMENT

Corporal punishment is a highly controversial issue in the United States today. Perhaps no other issue has drawn as much criticism as the use of physical punishment in public schools. Those who support corporal punishment contend that it facilitates changes in student behavior and teaches students self-discipline and respect for authority. Those who oppose corporal punishment view it as a legalized form of child abuse that conveys to students that violence is an acceptable method of resolving problems. Irrespective of the views supporting or opposing corporal punishment, the courts still view corporal punishment as an acceptable form of discipline when administered in a reasonable manner. Although corporal punishment is considered to be an acceptable form of discipline, school personnel are increasingly facing charges of assault and battery, prosecution, and even termination of employment for abusive acts against students.

Corporal punishment generally involves the use of physical contact for disciplinary purposes and is not uncommon within U.S. school systems. In fact, 19 states currently allow corporal punishment to be used as a means of discipline. Interestingly, the courts have sanctioned reasonable corporal punishment by school personnel under the concept of in loco parentis, but the laws in only one state protect school personnel who administer it.[*]

The question of the constitutionality of corporal punishment was reaffirmed in the 1977 landmark case *Ingraham v. Wright*, in which the U.S. Supreme Court ruled that even severe corporal punishment may not violate the Eighth Amendment prohibition of cruel and unusual punishment. This case arose when Ingraham and another student from

---

[*]The Alabama legislature passed a teacher immunity bill, Act 99-53, that provides immunity for teachers who use corporal punishment or otherwise maintain order when exercising such authority within their local boards.

the Dade County, Florida, public schools filed suit after they had been subjected to paddling. State law allowed corporal punishment if it was not "degrading or unduly severe" and if it was done after consultation with the principal or another teacher in charge of the school. For violating a teacher's instructions, Ingraham had received 20 licks while he was held over a table in the principal's office. He required medical attention and missed school for several days.

Although this paddling was "unduly severe," the High Court hearing the evidence and appeals found no Eighth Amendment constitutional violation, because that amendment does not deal with corporal punishment in public schools.

Although the court in *Ingraham* declined to declare corporal punishment as used in the context of public schools to be a violation of the cruel and unusual proscription or due process under federal law, it did state that paddling students deprived them of liberty interests protected by the Constitution. (See Chapter 5 for discussion of due process.) A prudent policy would require that an adult witness be present and that parents' wishes concerning this form of punishment be considered, if not respected.

Although the *Ingraham* case upholds the legality of corporal punishment as an acceptable means of controlling student behavior, local school district policy in many cases has seriously limited its use.

Reasonable Punishment

Poor decisions regarding the use of corporal punishment by school personnel may result in civil damage suits or even criminal prosecution for assault and battery. When it is permitted, corporal punishment should be used only as a measure of last resort. Every reasonable disciplinary measure should have been employed without success prior to its use. Collaboration among teachers, parents, and school officials to resolve a child's deviant behavior is viewed by some educators as a more positive alternative.

When corporal punishment is permitted, students should be informed beforehand of specific infractions that warrant its use. When administered, the punishment should be reasonable and consistent with the gravity of the infraction. Corporal punishment should never be administered excessively or with malice.

The courts have advanced two standards governing corporal punishment of students: The first is the reasonableness standard—punishment must be exerted within bounds of reason and humanity. The second is the good faith standard—the person administering the punishment must not be motivated by malice and must not inflict the punishment wantonly and excessively.[14]

Minimal Due Process

The student who is to be punished should be informed of the rule violation in question and provided an opportunity to respond. A brief, but thorough, informal hearing should be provided to allow the student an opportunity to present his or her side of the issue. Upon request, parents or guardians must be provided a written explanation of the reasons for the punishment and the name of the school official who was present to witness the punishment.

Excessive Punishment

Excessiveness occurs when the punishment is inflicted with such force or in such a manner that it is considered to be cruel and unusual. Excessiveness also occurs when no consideration is given to the age, size, gender, and physical condition of the student or the student's ability to bear the punishment. Assault and battery charges are typically associated with allegations of excessive punishment.

Although in loco parentis allows school personnel to administer corporal punishment, their actions must be considered reasonable and necessary under the circumstances. Corporal punishment should not be inflicted when students resist it. Teachers should be judicious in following school district policy in administering corporal punishment. Corporal punishment is very risky and could result in significant legal charges if administered improperly. It should be avoided if at all possible.

GUIDES

Corporal Punishment

1. Corporal punishment should not be used except for acts of misconduct that are so antisocial and disruptive in nature as to shock the conscience.
2. School personnel should not expect the courts to support malicious and excessive physical punishment of students.
3. Reasonable administration of corporal punishment should be based on such factors as the gravity of the

offense; the age, size, and gender of the student; and the physical ability of the child to bear the punishment.

4. If a student professes a lack of knowledge regarding the rule violation or innocence of the rule violation, a brief but adequate opportunity should be provided to explain the rule and allow the student to speak on his or her own behalf.

5. Whenever possible, students should be provided punishment options for deviant behavior. Corporal punishment should never be administered when the child is physically resisting.

6. Attempts should be made to comply with the parent's request that corporal punishment not be administered to the child, with the understanding that the parent assumes responsibility for the child's behavior during the school day.

CLASSROOM HARASSMENT

Sexual harassment may be considered a form of sexual discrimination. In *Davis v. Monroe County Board of Education*, the U.S. Supreme Court, in a stunning 5–4 decision, ruled that public schools may be sued for failing to deal with students who harass their classmates.[15] This landmark decision, hailed as a victory by sexual harassment protection groups, raises a number of interesting questions: How will it affect the operation and management of schools? Will it create insurmountable problems of supervision for teachers and principals? Will every adolescent gesture made against a classmate trigger a need for schools to respond? Has the High Court invoked a federal code of conduct that regulates behavior typically associated with adolescence? These are complex issues facing school leaders as they attempt to address harassment issues in their schools.

The U.S. Supreme Court's Decision Regarding Sexual Harassment

Justice Sandra Day O'Connor, writing for the majority in the 1999 *Davis v. Monroe County* case, which involved student-to-student sexual harassment, attempted to clarify these complex issues by indicating that lawsuits are valid only when the harassing student's behavior is so severe, pervasive, and objectively offensive that it denies the victim equal access to an education guaranteed by federal law. She further suggested that harassment claims are valid only when school administrators are clearly unreasonable and deliberately indifferent toward the alleged harassing conduct, which obviously means they must have been aware of such conduct and did nothing to address it. However, liability charges may be made even if a teacher is the only one aware of the harassing behavior.

GUIDES

Classroom Harassment

1. School district policies and procedures for employees and students should be formulated to address sexual harassment. Be certain that everyone—faculty, students, and staff—understands these policies and the consequences for violating them.
2. Educational programs should be provided periodically for faculty, staff, and students to familiarize them with all aspects of harassment and specific behaviors considered to fall in the harassment category.
3. Faculty and students should be encouraged to report all violations through a well-defined, developed, and publicized grievance procedure.
4. Educators should react swiftly and judiciously to complaints filed by students so that everyone is clear that the institution considers charges of harassment seriously.
5. An environment should be created in which students and school personnel feel comfortable in honestly reporting complaints of harassment, free from any form of reprisal.
6. The confidentiality of those filing complaints should be protected to the greatest degree possible. Professional reputations can be damaged if charges prove to be false.
7. A school climate should be created and maintained that is characterized by mutual respect and consideration of others.

REPORTING SUSPECTED CHILD ABUSE AND NEGLECT OCCURRING AT HOME

In virtually all states, teachers are required to report, to the appropriate agency, suspected cases of child abuse and neglect by a parent or guardian. School districts have adopted procedures for filing these reports. Forty-nine states have mandatory reporting requirements for teachers. If no evidence supports findings of abuse, teachers will not be liable. Immunity is granted in virtually every state when teachers make reports in good faith. Laws in most states penalize individuals who fail to report child abuse and neglect. Failure to report abuse is a misdemeanor that generally carries a fine of up to $1,000 and a jail sentence. Because teachers interact with their students daily, they are in a unique position to detect signs of abuse and neglect. Once abuse or neglect is suspected, teachers must report their suspicion through appropriate channels. Failure to do so may result in criminal liability.

PREGNANT STUDENTS

The courts have generally held that pregnant students may not be denied an opportunity to attend school. The basis for the court's position is that pregnant students must be afforded equal protection under the law, as well as due process of law.

Some school officials have attempted to force pregnant students to withdraw from school when they become aware that the student is pregnant, whereas other districts have specified a particular time for withdrawal. Many of these rules have been successful in the past. However, the courts have increasingly tended to declare these rules invalid. The commonly acceptable practice is that the student's physician may prescribe the time that the student should withdraw for health and safety reasons. On the student's withdrawal, school officials should provide appropriate homebound instruction. When cleared by the attending physician after childbirth, the student may return to school and is entitled to the same rights and privileges afforded other students.

MARRIED STUDENTS

Married students have the right to attend public schools. Any rules designed to exclude married students from attending school are invalid and in violation of their Fourteenth Amendment rights—namely, equal protection under the laws. School board rules that prohibited married students from permanently attending public schools were invalidated by the courts during the late 1920s and early 1930s.[16] School rules that required students to withdraw from school for a 1-year period after marriage were also invalidated by the court.[17] Further, the court established the position that a 16-year-old married student has the right to attend public school, even when she has a child.[18]

Married students are considered *emancipated*, that is, free of parental authority and control and free to make independent decisions and not subject to compulsory attendance laws. Thus, a married or minor student cannot be coerced to attend school. These students may attend as they wish.

There has been debate over the extent to which married students should be permitted to participate in extracurricular activities endorsed by the school. Although extracurricular activities have frequently been viewed as privileges that may or may not be granted by the board, this view has been invalidated on the basis that denying such privileges may violate equal protection and due process provisions of the Fourteenth Amendment.

GUIDES

Pregnant and Married Students

1. Pregnant and married students are afforded the same rights as all other students enrolled in public schools and may not be prohibited from attending school.
2. There must be compelling evidence demonstrating that the presence of married or pregnant students disrupts or interferes with school activities or has a negative influence on other students for a school official to justify any attempt to restrict those students' attendance.
3. The pregnant student's physician is authorized to determine when the student should withdraw and when it is feasible for her to return.
4. Homebound instruction should be offered for students who have withdrawn owing to pregnancy.
5. A heavy burden of proof rests with school officials when they attempt to exclude either pregnant or married students from participating in regular and extracurricular activities.
6. The courts are unanimous in invalidating school rules that prohibit married or pregnant students from attending school.

PRACTICAL TIPS

Do:

1. Recognize that students' rights cannot be restricted unless there is a defensible basis for the restriction. Maintaining a peaceful and orderly classroom is a defensible basis for imposing restrictions.

2. Stress the school's values, such as respect for others and civility, to students regarding the exercise of their rights to freedom of expression, as well as their obligations. Stressing school values can create a favorable learning environment.

3. Understand that students have a right to engage in an orderly protest as long as the students are respectful and do not disrupt the education process or violate school rules. Minor disruption must be permitted.

4. Exercise restraint in search decisions involving students, particularly those decisions related to personal searches. School or district policy must be stringently followed.

5. Respond to any allegations of classroom harassment among your students. Failure to do so could result in liability challenges and emotional harm to students who are victims of harassment.

Do not:

1. Abuse your authority in restricting students' rights to freedom of expression in matters relating to dress and appearance. Restrictions should not be imposed on the basis of your own personal views regarding appropriate style and fashion. Immodest, disruptive, or unsanitary grooming, as well as safety concerns, may be reasonably addressed. School district policy should provide guidance in this area.

2. Use indefensible disciplinary practices that may result in embarrassment or mental anguish for your students. Students may experience irreparable emotional trauma from verbal abuse, especially in the presence of their peers.

3. Fail to report suspected cases of child abuse and neglect that originate outside the school. Failure to do so may result in personal liability for the educator, as well as in fines.

4. Treat married or pregnant students differently than any other students. They enjoy the same rights and privileges as all other students.

ENDNOTES

1. *Tinker v. Des Moines Independent Community School District*, 393 U.S. 503, at 511, 89 S. Ct. 733, 21 L. Ed. 2d 731 (1969).
2. *Blackwell v. Issaquena County Board of Education,* 366 F.2d 749 (5th Cir. 1966).

3. *Bethel School District v. Fraser*, 478 U.S. 675, 106 S. Ct. 3159, 92 L. Ed. 2d 549 (1986).

4. *Hazelwood School District v. Kuhlmeier*, 484 U.S. 260 at 276; 108 S. Ct. 562; 98 L. Ed. 2d 592 (1987).

5. *Karr v. Schmidt*, 460 F.2d 609 (5th Cir. 1972).

6. *Morse v. Frederick*, 439 F.3d 1114 (9th Cir. 2006).

7. *Guiles v. Marineau*, 461 F.3d (2d Cir. 2006).

8. *New Jersey v. T.L.O.*, 469 U.S. 809; 105 S. Ct. 68; 83 L. Ed. 2d 19 (1984).

9. *Bellnier v. Lund*, 438 F. Supp. 47 (N.D.N.Y. 1977).

10. *Desilets v. Clearview Regional Board of Education*, 137 N.J. 585, 647 A.2d 150 (1994).

11. *Zamoro v. Pomeroy*, 639 F.2d 662 (10th Cir. 1981).

12. *Jones v. Latexo Independent School District*, 499 F. Supp. 223 (E.D. Tex. 1080).

13. *Powers v. Plumas Unified School District*, 192 F.3d 1260 (9th Cir. 1999).

14. Ibid.

15. *Davis v. Monroe County Board of Education*, 526, U.S. 629; 110 S. Ct. 1661; 143 L. Ed. 2d 839 (1999).

16. *McLeod v. State*, 122 So. 77 (Miss. 1929).

17. *Board of Education of Harrodsburg v. Bentley*, 383 S.W.2d 387 (Tex. 1967).

18. *Alvin Independent School District v. Cooper*, 404 S.W.2d 76 (Tex. 1966).

5

Due Process and Student Safety

Since the No Child Left Behind (NCLB) Act was enacted, school safety has become a major priority for local school districts. Districts must provide assurance that plans are on file regarding steps schools will initiate to maintain safe and drug-free environments. In March 2003, U.S. Secretary of Education Rod Paige announced that $30 million was available in fiscal 2003 to assist school districts in improving and strengthening emergency response and crisis management plans. Additionally, the National School Safety Center (NSSC) was created to provide assistance in combating school safety problems so that schools could be free to focus on the primary job of educating the nation's children. NSSC was established by presidential directive in 1984 as a partnership between the U.S. Departments of Justice and Education.

CREATING SAFE SCHOOLS

Just as the nation faces threats of terrorism that affect the health and safety of all citizens, U.S. schools also face safety threats that affect the welfare of students. Maintaining safe schools has become a major challenge for school officials during the past decade. School shootings (in Pearl, Mississippi; West Paducah, Kentucky; Jonesboro, Arkansas; Edinboro, Pennsylvania; Springfield, Oregon; Littleton, Colorado; Conyers, Georgia; Knoxville, Tennessee; Red Lake, Minnesota; and Newtown, Connecticut [the worst in U.S. history]) have increased pressures on school leaders to provide a safe learning environment where teachers can effectively perform their instructional duties. A survey conducted in 2012 by the U.S. Department of Education revealed that at least 10% of schools in the United States are facing problems of violence and at least one serious crime other than theft or physical attacks. A minority of the student body appears to have a predisposition toward violence, based on their inability to control personal anger. Bullying, insulting, or disrespectful behavior has often results in fights. During the 2009–10 school year, 85% of public schools recorded one or more of these incidents of violence, theft, or other crimes, totaling an estimated 1.9 million crimes. This figure translates to a rate of approximately 40 crimes per 1,000 students enrolled in 2009–10. During the same year, 60% of schools reported one of the specified crimes to the police, totaling about 689,000 crimes—or 15 crimes per 1,000 students enrolled.[1] If access to guns is added, there is a greater probability of violent outcomes. Another major threat to school safety is the presence of youth gangs in schools, although gang presence in public schools appears to be decreasing. Nevertheless, gangs still pose a major challenge for school leaders.

With the presence of gangs in schools, school leaders are encountering pressures from parents, citizens, and school boards to provide a safe environment where teachers can teach and students can learn. Added to these pressures is the court's view that schools are "safe places," based on the assumption that children are supervised by licensed and well-trained teachers and administrators. Because schools are presumed to be safe, failure to provide a safe environment can prove costly when evidence reveals that school leaders failed to act responsibly in protecting students when they knew or should have known of impending danger.

Young people join gangs for various reasons, including peer pressure; neglect at home; economic reward; the need for recognition; the desire for excitement, identity, and acceptance; and the lack of appropriate involvement in school activities. Gang members demonstrate strong loyalty to their gang and will do whatever is necessary to be initiated into the gang, including committing violent crimes. In some instances, the lack of success in school and a feeling of alienation contribute to gang affiliation.

Gangs are forces that are challenging schools and communities across the nation. School leaders, however, have an especially important role to play, because gang violence has quickly become a part of public schools' vocabulary.

GANGS AND DRESS

Gang members tend to wear specific apparel or colors to convey gang affiliation. Wherever gang activity has been prevalent in the school or community and there is clear knowledge that certain types of dress are associated with disruptive gang activity, school leaders may prohibit such dress. In all cases, such prohibitions should be preceded by the publication of school policies that clearly communicate the need to regulate this type of dress.

In most cases, the pattern or style of dress is generally chosen by gang leaders. As pressure is exerted by parents, law enforcement officers, and school officials, gangs will often change their appearance to become less recognizable. Today many gang members wear professional sports team jackets, caps, and T-shirts, making it more difficult to identify them. Because school officials are responsible for protecting students from potential danger, they may take reasonable steps to minimize gang presence in school. Conversely, school officials should provide opportunities for all students to succeed in school and feel that they are important members of the school's family.

GUIDES

Gangs and Dress

1. Efforts should be made to ensure that school personnel have knowledge of gang identification strategies as well as gang management techniques.
2. Policies and procedures should be established to address gang violence in the school.
3. A system should be implemented to report suspected gang involvement and activity to proper law enforcement gang units.
4. Dress related to gang activity may be banned by school officials.

School Uniform Dress Policies and Students' Rights to Freedom of Expression

Many school officials, in their desire to create and maintain safe schools, have developed student uniform dress code policies. These policies are intended to provide easy identification of students, eliminate gang dress, promote discipline, deter theft and violence, prevent unauthorized visitors from intruding on campus, and foster a positive learning environment. Although there is no national consensus regarding the effectiveness of school uniforms, their use is increasing in schools across the nation as part of an overall program to improve school safety and discipline.

Early Legal Challenges

With frequent acts of violence occurring in public schools, school districts are moving swiftly and aggressively to enforce uniform dress policies. Early legal battles have already surfaced regarding dress codes. A sixth grader in Alabama was banned from wearing a gold cross unless it was out of sight inside her shirt. The case was settled out of court when the district revised its dress code to include religious accommodations. A school board in New Mexico devised a dress code prohibiting trench coats, knee-high boots, black clothing, spiked jewelry, and upside-down crosses, including religious symbols. Parents objected to the religious ban. The district refused to lift the ban, and the case was turned over to the American Civil Liberties Union (ACLU) to mount a lawsuit against the district. The Ohio chapter of the ACLU assisted a student who desired to wear a shirt with "Born to Raze Hell" on the front and "I'm the Christian the Devil Warned You About" on the back. A settlement was eventually reached. These legal cases suggest that there may be some lack of sensitivity to the First Amendment rights of students as school uniform policies are drafted.

GUIDES

Uniforms

1. Parents, teachers, community leaders, and student representatives should be involved in drafting school uniform policies.
2. Students' religious expressions must be protected in relation to uniform dress codes.
3. Students' rights to freedom of expression should be protected within reasonable limits as uniform dress standards are established.
4. School uniform policies should be enforced fairly and consistently.
5. School uniform policies should be implemented as a component of an overall school safety program.
6. School uniform policies should be reviewed and revised as the need arises.

ZERO TOLERANCE AND SCHOOL SAFETY

School safety has become a leading priority for school leaders across the nation as they respond to a wave of violence that has struck public schools throughout the United States. Although schools are still considered safe places, limiting violence has quickly become a major challenge for school officials. Many districts have initiated a zero tolerance policy in an effort to reduce school violence. Opponents are raising questions as to whether school leaders are going too far and moving too swiftly with a "one strike, you're out" approach. They also are questioning whether school leaders' actions are reasonable and legally defensible.

Recent Zero Tolerance Practices

Since zero tolerance policies have emerged in a number of districts, students have been affected in ways that raise questions regarding the legal defensibility of such an approach. For example, a third-grade girl was expelled for a year because her grandmother sent a birthday cake, and a knife for cutting the cake, to school. A straight-A student was ordered to attend "reform school" after a classmate dropped a pocketknife in his lap. An Eagle Scout was suspended for 3 weeks for having an emergency supply kit in his car that included a pocketknife.

Although zero tolerance has sometimes been misapplied, the policy may be effective in addressing drugs, weapons, school violence, and disruptions that threaten students' safety. Ideally, zero tolerance should focus on serious and documented offenses that threaten safety as well as an orderly school environment.

Unquestionably, school officials are concerned about school safety owing to past incidents of violence in schools. However, their concerns should be tempered with sound reason and a regard for the rights of students. Policies that do not weigh the severity of the offense, the student's history of past behavior, due process, or alternative education for students involved in long-term expulsion are, at best, highly risky legally. Interestingly, according to the American Psychological Association (APA), research has not found any evidence that zero tolerance policies have a deterrent effect or keep schools safe. Many school districts are reexamining their zero tolerance policies.

GUIDES

Zero Tolerance

1. Zero tolerance policies should not be used solely to rid the school of disruptive students.
2. Teachers, parents, community leaders, and student representatives should be involved in the formulation of zero tolerance policies.
3. Policies should be formulated with the recognition that students possess constitutional rights.

4. Zero tolerance should not be considered a cure-all for student misconduct.
5. The student's history of behavior in school, the seriousness of the offense, and whether there is an immediate need to take disciplinary action should be considered before administering punishment.
6. The student's substantive and procedural rights should be safeguarded in all disciplinary matters.

BULLYING IN PUBLIC SCHOOLS

Bullying in public schools has become a serious and escalating problem. Each day thousands of children attending school face harassment and humiliation by bullies. Victims of bullying experience psychological and, often, physical scars for a lifetime. Bullying typically involves repeated, unprovoked harassment of another individual in which the victim has difficulty defending him- or herself. Students have the right to be educated in an environment free of fear. When bullying incidents occur, they disrupt students' learning and academic performance. Teachers and administrators have a legal duty to reasonably protect students from intimidation and threats to their safety, because they serve *in loco parentis* (in place of parents) while children are assigned to their care during the school day as well as during extended school activities. Suspected cases of bullying should be taken seriously and investigated to ensure that students are protected and schools do not face potential liability for failure to respond to bullying behavior.

Cyberbullying

Cyberbullying has escalated in recent years. *Cyberbullying* involves the use of electronic devices to send or post hurtful, embarrassing text or images intended to create anxiety, intimidation, or emotional distress in another person. Cyberbullying may involve a pattern of continuing unwelcome emails or text messages to others who have indicated they wish to have no contact with the sender. More serious forms of communication may involve hate speech, threats, sexually offensive content, or messages designed to ridicule the victim. Posting false statements on the Internet or on social media networks also falls within the spectrum of offensive communication. In some instances, an individual's personal or sensitive information may be disclosed for the purpose of defaming or embarrassing the victim. A continued pattern of these types of communications constitutes *cyberstalking*.

Megan Meier Cyberbullying Prevention Act

Megan Meier, a 13-year-old student, committed suicide after a classmate and her mother fabricated an online account attributed to a fictitious 16-year-old boy to whom Megan was attracted. Megan thought messages were cordial and inviting at the outset, but they later turned negative about her and were communicated to her friends along with bulletins suggesting that she was a bad person.

Based on Megan Meier's unfortunate suicide incident stemming from cyberbullying through a social network website, in 2009 Congress introduced H.R. 1966, known as the Megan Meier Cyberbullying Prevention Act. The intent of this act is to amend the federal criminal code to impose criminal penalties on anyone who transmits in interstate or foreign commerce a communication intended to coerce, intimidate, harass, or cause substantial emotional distress to another person, using electronic means to support severe, repeated, and hostile behavior. A subcommittee hearing was held on September 30, 2009. The bill has not passed out of the House Committee on the Judiciary as of this writing.

GUIDES

Bullying

1. Teachers have a duty to protect students from harassing and humiliating acts by bullies.
2. All students have a right to receive an education in an environment free of fear.
3. Teachers may face liability claims if they fail to respond to observable acts of bullying that result in injury to victims.

SCHOOL SUSPENSION

School suspension is a legal form of discipline for students who violate school or district policy. In-school suspensions are used by a number of school districts in the United States. However, out-of-school suspensions remain the most prevalent. Race, ethnicity, and socioeconomic status are often factors that influence school suspension decisions, according to a study by the Applied Research Center, a nationally based research, education, and policy institute in Oakland, California. There appears to be a close relationship between socioeconomic status, race, and ethnicity and the rate of suspensions. Every year, larger numbers of minority students, who typically have lower socioeconomic status than their peers, are suspended.

School suspensions require that procedural and substantive provisions of due process be met. Basically, *due process* is a course of legal proceedings following established rules that assure the enforcement and protection of individual rights. The essential element of due process is fundamental fairness, which means a fair hearing and a fair, impartial judgment.

DISCIPLINE INVOLVING MINORITY STUDENTS

Racial Disparities in Policy Enforcement

The issue of evident racial disparity in the application of discipline policies among students is creating significant concerns for the Office for Civil Rights of the U.S. Department of Education. For example, in many of the nation's middle schools, black males are nearly three times as likely to be suspended as white males, according to a new study that also discovered that black females are suspended at four times the rate of white females. School authorities are suspending Hispanic and American Indian middle school students at higher rates than white students, though not at such disproportionate rates as for black students.[2] These racial disparities have become so profound that it has prompted the Office of Civil Rights to provide guidance that will include an analysis of disparate impact. The civil rights enforcement process will involve seeking evidence of "different" treatment or evidence of school personnel intentionally discriminating against a particular group of students. The department will also assess disparate impact to determine the extent to which a particular group is disproportionately affected by a policy, although no intention of discrimination may exist. This statistical analysis will also determine whether school policies intend to discriminate in their application of disciplinary practices.

GUIDES

School Suspension

1. Adequate notice must be provided students and parents regarding the existence of rules governing student behavior. These should be clearly communicated to all affected by their implementation.
2. A record should be compiled that includes the following information:
   a. description of the infraction allegedly committed,
   b. time of the alleged infraction,
   c. place the alleged infraction occurred,

d. those person(s) who witnessed the alleged act, and

e. previous efforts made to remedy the alleged misbehavior.

3. Students should be provided either oral or written notice of charges against them, the evidence school authorities possess to support the charges, and an opportunity to refute the charges.

4. Because permanent removal is not intended, no delay is necessary between the time notice is given and the time of the actual hearing. In most instances, school officials and students may informally discuss the alleged misconduct immediately after it is reported.

5. During the hearing, the school official should listen to all sides of the issue. There should be adequate time provided for the accused students to present their side of the issue, without interruption.

6. Parents or guardians should be informed of the hearing and provided written notification of the action that results from the hearing.

7. Policy committees consisting of diverse groups of parents, community leaders, educators, and students should be formed to analyze existing policies and identify those that tend to create the potential for unintended discrimination against minority students, particularly zero tolerance policies if they exist.

8. Partnerships with parents should be established to focus on children who may be experiencing significant behavioral problems at school.

9. Alternative consequences should be sought to minimize suspending or expelling students, such as parent conferences, Saturday detention, and alternative school placements.

10. A school environment should be established and maintained so that every child feels important irrespective of ability, socioeconomic background, or academic achievement.

Procedural and Substantive Due Process

Due process consists of two essential aspects: procedural and substantive. Students as citizens are entitled to rights associated with both aspects. *Procedural* due process requires that certain legal procedures be followed to ensure fundamental fairness and to avoid arbitrary and capricious actions by school officials, whereas *substantive* due process deals with the student's individual, or personal, rights.

Procedural due process requires that a legally defensible procedure be followed to ensure that proper safeguards are available to protect those whose rights are in jeopardy. Substantive due process suggests that when a student's right is restricted, a valid reason must be established to justify such restriction, and the actual means employed to deny the student's right must be reasonably calculated. The significance of substantive and procedural requirements is that both provisions must be met by school officials to satisfy the basic requirements of the Fourteenth Amendment.

EXPULSION

Unlike suspension, expulsion is considered one of the more severe forms of discipline because it involves long-term separation from the school district or, in some instances, permanent separation. Expulsion usually involves more serious offenses or rule violations than does suspension. In recent years, a significant number of expulsions have been linked with weapons violations. Because expulsion is a form of discipline that deprives the student of the right to attend school, it must be preceded by a formal hearing in which the student is afforded full Fourteenth Amendment rights involving due process and equal protection privileges.

The threat of expulsion is so serious that students and parents should be aware of infractions that may result in expulsion. These infractions should be identified by school and district policy. Additionally, they should be clearly communicated to students and parents to ensure that there is no misinterpretation regarding the intent and substance of expulsion policies.

In virtually every state, the board of education is the only entity with legal authority to expel students. The board or a designated body is responsible for holding the expulsion hearing and meeting all rudiments of due process consistent with the Fourteenth Amendment. Any errors along procedural or substantive grounds usually will result in the student's position being supported by the courts in a legal contest.

GUIDES

Expulsion

1. Students, and parents or legal guardians, should be informed, in accordance with school or district policy, of specific infractions that may result in expulsion. They

should also be informed of their Fourteenth Amendment rights regarding substantive and procedural due process.

2. In cases of serious misconduct for which stringent disciplinary measures may be imposed, the student is entitled to written notice of the charges, and a right to a fair hearing. Written notice must be furnished to the student and to the parent or legal guardian well in advance of the hearing.

3. At a minimum, a written notice of charges must be delivered, and the correct procedural steps should be taken that allow the student the following rights:
   a. right to a fair hearing,
   b. right to inspect evidence,
   c. right to present evidence on his or her own behalf,
   d. right to legal counsel,
   e. right to call witnesses,
   f. right to cross-examination and confrontation,
   g. right to avoid self-incrimination, and
   h. right to appeal.

METAL DETECTORS

Metal detectors have grown in use and popularity as school officials seek to maintain a safe and orderly school environment. To date no legal challenge has reached the U.S. Supreme Court regarding the use of metal detectors. However, there has been litigation at the district and appellate court levels. For example, In *In re F.B.*, a student was subjected to an entry search on arrival at his high school in Philadelphia, Pennsylvania. Parents and students were informed at the beginning of the year that metal detector searches would occur, and postings would be made throughout the year. Students' packs and coats were searched by a handheld metal detector. Officers involved were acting under the direction of school officials. F.B. emptied his pockets. He was found to be carrying a Swiss army knife with a 3-inch blade and was arrested. The court held that there was no Fourth Amendment violation, because the search affected a limited privacy interest, the search was minimally intrusive, notice of the search had been provided, and the purpose of the search was compelling. No finding of individualized suspicion was necessary because the search was conducted on all students. The judge ruled that in the subsequent trial, the evidence disclosed by the search should not be suppressed.[3]

A New York court in *People v. Dukes* was the first to legalize the use of metal detectors in public schools. These searches involved weapons. Since *Dukes*, other lower courts have heard cases in Los Angeles, Chicago, Philadelphia, Louisiana, Texas, Delaware, Illinois, Kentucky, Florida, Georgia, Missouri, South Carolina, and Tennessee.[4]

The use of metal detection, like other intrusive methods, must be justified as reasonable and necessary to meet a legitimate school objective. In the F.B. case, maintaining a safe and orderly school environment was considered a legitimate school objective. In all cases, there should be significant or compelling evidence to suggest that metal detectors need to be used. For example, if a school has a chronic history of drug abuse and violence involving the use of weapons, the courts will likely support the use of metal detectors as a means of combating these problems. If metal detectors are employed by the school officials, students should be informed before the procedure is implemented that they are subject to this type of screening. Such information should be included in school or district policy and clearly communicated to students and parents. In no instance, except in extreme emergencies, should students be surprised by the use of metal detectors. Last, if detectors are used, the methods of employing them must be reasonable and not designed to degrade students.

GUIDES

Metal Detectors

1. Metal detectors should be used only when there is evidence of student behavior that poses a threat to the health and safety of students in the school. Barring an emergency, students and parents should be informed beforehand that metal detection will be employed and should also be informed of the basis for employing this method.
2. If metal detectors are used to achieve a legitimate school interest, their use will likely be supported by the courts.
3. Students and parents should be informed through a legally defensible school policy regarding the use of metal detectors.
4. If school officials' acts are reasonable regarding the use of metal detectors, they will generally receive the support of the courts.

DRUG TESTING

Until the mid-1990s, no case involving drug testing in public schools had been litigated by the U.S. Supreme Court. The case *Vernonia School District v. Acton,* however, reached the Supreme Court in 1995 when the U.S. Court of Appeals for the Ninth Circuit reversed the district court's holding for the school district. School officials in Oregon formulated a district policy based on the belief that some athletes had been smoking marijuana and using other drugs. They also believed that drugs were a major factor in the formation of rowdy student groups. Under the school district's policy, all student athletes were required to provide a urine sample at the beginning of the season for the particular sport in which they participated. Athletes who tested positive were offered the choice to either undergo counseling and weekly testing or face suspension from athletics for the current and subsequent seasons. This policy was challenged by a prospective athlete.

The Supreme Court held that the Vernonia School District's program was reasonable and constitutionally permissible for three reasons. First, students, especially student athletes, have low expectations for privacy in communal locker rooms and restrooms where students must produce their urine samples. Second, the testing program was designed to be unobtrusive, with students producing their samples in relative privacy and with the samples handled confidentially by an outside laboratory. Finally, the program served the school district's interest in combating drug abuse.[5] Some courts have recently supported warrantless drug testing programs for students involved in extracurricular activities.

Another case, *Board of Ed. of Independent School Dist. No. 92 of Pottawatomie Cty. v. Earls*, involved a warrantless search involving urine samples of students participating in extracurricular activities. The U.S. Supreme Court upheld the drug testing policy as one that promoted student health and safety in light of the fact that the school district was experiencing a drug problem.[6]

ALCOHOL USE AND BREATHALYZERS

School districts would be well advised to develop policies that discourage students from abusing alcohol. These policies should be sufficiently definite so as to inform students of expectations regarding alcohol use on school property or at any school-sponsored event. School officials should exercise caution and avoid conducting random testing of students. Such practice would be considered arbitrary, capricious, and indefensible.

Students should not be subjected to any type of test unless reasonable suspicion has been established that points to either a single student or a group of students who are thought to be under the influence of alcohol. Even then, caution should be exercised to ensure that Breathalyzer tests are conducted in privacy and not in a manner that embarrasses the student.

Breathalyzer policies should be designed to deter students from using alcohol. An alcohol education course may be valuable in informing students of the health risks associated with alcohol use as well as risks associated with becoming dependent on alcohol. Teachers have a responsibility to report any student believed to be under the influence of alcohol. School officials should consult school or district policy for guidance in conducting Breathalyzer tests.

GUIDES

Drugs and Alcohol Testing

1. A district-wide program on drug education and alcohol abuse should be initiated, stressing the harmful effects of such substances and urging abstention from their use.
2. School and district policies should be developed prohibiting the use and/or possession of alcohol or drugs on school grounds and indicating specific actions that will be taken when students are found guilty of violating school and district policy.
3. A full due process procedure should be implemented to ensure that there is a fair and impartial hearing in which students can present their side of the issue if they are accused of drug or alcohol abuse.
4. Teachers, parents, students, health officials, and community citizens should be involved in formulating school and/or district policies regarding drug testing programs that are reasonable and legally defensible.
5. Support should be provided if students are found guilty of drug abuse. This is a time when students need as much support as possible.
6. Open relationships should be maintained with parents so that frequent communication can occur, especially in cases where there is a suspicion that a student may be involved with illicit drugs.

PRACTICAL TIPS

Do:

1. Understand that teachers are expected to create a safe school environment for students under their care.
2. Recognize that students are entitled to procedural and substantive due process provisions in cases involving

school infractions. Violation of due process rights will not be upheld by the courts and will usually violate school or district policy.

3. Recognize that an unreasonable exercise of teachers' authority will not receive support from the courts. Courts consistently support prudent teachers who use good judgment in matters involving students.

Do not:

1. Make arbitrary decisions regarding student misconduct. School or district policy will provide direction in student disciplinary matters.

2. Allow observable bullying behavior by students in the classroom or the school. Bullying has resulted in both physical and emotional injury to students and may result in teacher liability, depending on facts and circumstances.

3. Ignore evidence of gang activity in the school. Proactive measures are necessary to limit gang presence. Many students who affiliate with gangs experience minimal success in school and feel alienated from the school.

4. Fail to maintain open communication with parents regarding student misconduct in your classroom. Parental involvement can be pivotal in controlling undesirable academic and student behavior.

ENDNOTES

1. National Center for Education Statistics, U.S. Department of Education, Institute of Educational Sciences, 2010.
2. Dillon, Sam (2010, September 13). Racial disparity in school suspension. *The New York Times.*
3. *In re F.B.*, 658 A.2d 1378 (Pa. Super. Ct. 1995), *aff'd* 726 A.2d 361 (Pa. 1999).
4. *People v. Dukes*, 580 N.Y.S.2d 850 (N.Y. City Crim. Ct. 1992).
5. *Veronia School District v. Acton*, 115 S. Ct. 2386; 132 L. Ed. 2d 564 (1995).
6. *Board of Ed. of Independent School Dist. No. 92 of Pottawatomie Cty. v. Earls* (01-332) 536 U.S. 822 (2002); 242 F.3d 1264, reversed.

6

Liability and
Student Records

The primary purpose of maintaining education records should be to aid school personnel in developing the best education program for each student enrolled in the school. An effective student file contains information used for counseling, program development, individualized instruction, grade placement, college admissions, and a variety of other purposes. In addition to certain types of directory information, student files typically include family background information, health records, progress reports, achievement test results, psychological data, disciplinary records, and other confidential material.

Public Law 93-380, the Family Educational Rights and Privacy Act (FERPA), protects confidentiality of student records. This act, commonly referred to as the Buckley Amendment, was enacted by Congress in 1974 to guarantee parents and students a certain degree of confidentiality and fundamental fairness with respect to the maintenance and use of student records. The law is designed to ensure that certain types of personally identifiable information regarding students will not be released without parental consent. If a student is at least 18 years of age or attends a postsecondary institution, parental consent is not required. In those events, the student has the authority to provide consent. If the student 18 years old or older is a dependent for tax purposes, parents retain a coextensive access right. Because P.L. 93-380 is a federal statute, it applies to school districts and schools that receive federal funds. Schools should develop relevant policies and procedures, including a listing of the types and locations of their education records and persons who are responsible for maintaining these records. Copies of these policies and procedures should be made available to parents or students on request.

SANCTIONS FOR VIOLATING FAMILY
PRIVACY RIGHTS

An excerpt of the Buckley Act states the following:

> *No funds shall be available under any program to any education agency or institution which has a policy of denying access or which effectively prevents the parents of students who are or have been in attendance at a school of such agency, the right to inspect and review the educational records of their children.*[1]

At a minimum, the school district should provide, on an annual basis, to parents, guardians, and eligible students, information regarding the content of the law and should inform them of their rights to file complaints with the Family Policy Compliance Office of the Department of Education. If non-English-speaking parents are affected, the district has a responsibility to notify them in their native language.[2] Annual notification must include the following information:

1. the right to inspect and review education records;
2. the right to seek amendment of records believed to be inaccurate, misleading, or in violation of the student's privacy;
3. consent to disclose personally identifiable information contained in the student's records, except where the Buckley Act authorizes disclosure without consent; and
4. the right to file with the department a complaint, under §99.63 and §99.64, concerning alleged failures by the education agency or institution to comply with requirements of the Buckley Amendment.

In addition, the following should be included in the annual notification to students and parents:

1. procedures for exercising the right to inspect and review education records;
2. procedures for requesting amendments of records;
3. specification of criteria for determining who constitutes a school official and what constitutes a legitimate education interest.

Furthermore, an education agency or institution has a duty to effectively notify parents or eligible students who are disabled. Additionally, parents, guardians, or eligible students should be provided information regarding procedures for accessing education records if they desire to review them. Table 6.1 lists the content of education records.

TABLE 6.1   Content of Education Records

Education Records Include	Education Records Do Not Include
1. Records	1. Instructional records
2. Files	2. Supervisory records
3. Documents	3. Records maintained by law enforcement units for law enforcement purposes

4. Other material that
  a. contains information directly related to a student;
  b. is maintained by an education agency, institution, or person acting for an agency or institution
	4. Records on an 18-year-old student attending a postsecondary institution, that are maintained by a physician, psychiatrist, psychologist, or other recognized professional or paraprofessional involved in the treatment of the student

Source: P.L. 93–380

The school district may release directory information regarding students, provided that such information is
published yearly in a public newspaper. Directory information typically includes the following:

1. name;
2. address;
3. telephone number;
4. date and place of birth;
5. participation in extracurricular activities;
6. weight, height, and membership on athletic teams;
7. dates of attendance; and
8. diploma and awards received.

If any parents or guardians object to the release of directory information on their child, their objection should be
noted in the record and honored by the school district.

School policy should define what items are considered
directory information and the circumstances under which this
information should be released. Except for directory information, all personally identifiable records directly related to the
student shall be kept confidential, unless the parent or guardian signs a consent form releasing certain such information.

Rights of Parents

Parents or legal guardians have the right to inspect their child's record. A school official should be present to assist a parent or guardian in interpreting information contained in the files and to respond to questions that may be raised during the review of the files. Parents or legal guardians also may challenge the accuracy of any information found in the files regarding their child. The school must schedule a conference within a reasonable period after the request (10 days or less, although the act calls for no more than 45 days), with appropriate personnel, to discuss the information that may be deemed inaccurate, inappropriate, or misleading. If agreement is reached to the satisfaction of the parents, no further action is necessary. Appropriate deletions or corrections are executed, recorded in the student file, and communicated to parents or guardians in written form.

If the conference does not result in changes to the satisfaction of parents, they may request a hearing with the director of pupil personnel or a designee to appeal the decision reached during the conference. Ideally, the hearing should be scheduled within 10 days or less after the conference. The parent or guardian may be represented by legal counsel. A final decision should be rendered within 10 days subsequent to the hearing. If the school official hearing the case decides that the information is accurate and correct, the parent must be informed and provided an opportunity to place statements of disagreement in the file, together with reasons for the disagreement. This explanation must become a permanent part of the record and must be disclosed when the records are released. The parent or guardian may also seek relief in civil court.

When consent is necessary to release student records, it must be provided in written form and signed and dated by the consenting person. The consent form should include a specification of the records to be released, reason for the release, and the names of the individuals to whom the records will be released. Once confidential records are received by the requesting party, school officials who are releasing the records should emphasize that the information they contain is not to be divulged to other parties without the express permission of the parents, guardians, or eligible students. Parents, guardians, or eligible students must be notified before a school or district complies with a judicial order requesting education records. School officials in another school district in which a student plans to enroll may access that student's records, provided parents or guardians are notified in advance that the records are being transferred to the new district.

Rights of Noncustodial Parents

Occasionally, controversy arises regarding the rights of a noncustodial biological parent to access his or her child's education records. School officials often find themselves caught between a custodial parent's request that the noncustodial parent not be permitted to access the child's records and the request of the noncustodial parent to do so. School or district policy normally provides guidance in these situations. A noncustodial case arose in New York when the mother of a child requested that the school not allow the child's father to see their son's education records. The father challenged the school's refusal to allow him access to the child's records. The district court ruled that neither parent could be denied access to the child's records under the Family Educational Rights and Privacy Act. The court held that schools should make education records accessible to both parents of any child fortunate enough to have both parents interested in the child's welfare.[3]

Rights of Eligible Students

As previously mentioned, the student may exercise the same rights afforded parents or guardians if he or she has reached the age of 18 or is enrolled in a postsecondary institution. The student may inspect confidential records and also challenge the accuracy of information contained in the file. Additionally, the student may determine whether anyone other than authorized individuals may have access to personal files. Students also have a right to receive a copy of their personal file if they choose to have one. Eligible students are afforded the same due process provisions as parents are offered if they choose to challenge the accuracy of information contained in their file. They may also, under certain conditions, bring liability charges against school personnel for defamation (discussed later in this chapter).

Rights of School Personnel

Teachers, counselors, and administrators who have a legitimate education interest in viewing records may do so. A written form, which must be maintained permanently with the file, should indicate specifically what files were reviewed by school personnel and the date on which the files were reviewed. Each person desiring access to the file is required to sign this written form. These forms should be available for parents, guardians, or eligible students, because they remain permanently with the file. If challenged, school personnel must demonstrate a legitimate reason for having reviewed the student's file.

In 1994, FERPA was amended to emphasize that institutions are not prohibited from maintaining records related to a disciplinary action taken against a student for behavior that posed a significant risk to the student or others. Likewise, institutions are not prevented from disclosing such information to school officials who have been determined to have a legitimate education interest in the behavior of the student. School districts also are permitted to disclose information regarding disciplinary actions to school officials in other schools that have a legitimate educational interest in the behavior of students.

Enforcement of State and Federal Statutes

Federal and state officials may inspect files without parental consent to enforce federal or state laws or to audit or evaluate federal education programs. In these cases, personally identifiable information may not be associated with any student records, unless Congress, by law, specifically authorizes federal officials to gather personally identifiable data. Information may also be released without consent in connection with applications for student financial aid. Authorized representatives who may access records include (1) the comptroller general of the United States, (2) the secretary of state, (3) an administrative head of an education agency, and (4) state and education authorities. School district policies should address these issues so that parents or guardians, as well as eligible students, are informed of these exceptions. Another significant exception involves student health information.

The Health Insurance Portability and Accountability Act (HIPAA) and FERPA protect individuals from risks regarding the privacy of their personal health information. HIPAA ensures that personal health information will not be inappropriately accessed, researched, or misused. However, HIPAA's definition of protected health information excludes education records protected by FERPA. Therefore, health information contained in student records is exempt from HIPAA's requirements.

FAMILY EDUCATION RIGHTS AND PRIVACY ACT

Significant U.S. Supreme Court Ruling

On February 19, 2002, the U.S. Supreme Court ruled in *Owasso ISD v. Falvo*[4] that peer grading does not violate FERPA. The U.S. Department of Education has reviewed the court's ruling and may issue additional guidance or regulations to further clarify the scope of the term *education records*.

DEFAMATION BY SCHOOL PERSONNEL

Defamation and resulting liability applies to the misuse of student records. When a teacher communicates to an unauthorized person personal and sensitive information about a student that results in injury to the student's reputation or standing in the school, or that diminishes the respect and esteem with which the student is regarded, that teacher may face charges of libel or slander, depending upon the manner and intent in which such information is communicated.

Defamation is a tort, or civil, wrong. It occurs when false statements are made about another person with the intent to harm that person's good name and reputation or to subject the person to hatred, contempt, or ridicule.

Slander

Slander is oral defamation, which occurs when school personnel inadvertently communicate sensitive and damaging information contained in student files to others who have no need to be informed. Libel and slander involve communication to a third party. Information contained in student files is there for the exclusive use of the teacher, principal, or counselor who has a legitimate interest in accessing this information as each works with the student. Information should not be accessed unless there is a valid education-related objective to be met by a review of the information.

Once the information is obtained, it should be used only in providing and improving educational opportunities for the student. By no means should confidential information be discussed in a canny, amusing, or facetious manner. Under no circumstances should the student be ridiculed. The law is very specific in indicating that personally identifiable information should not be communicated to third parties without proper consent. When this is done, not only is the law violated, but the educator runs the risk of defaming the student. Off-the-cuff remarks and sharing sensitive information regarding a student's personal file are absolutely prohibited and may result in liability damages against those who are guilty of committing these acts.

School personnel are well advised to maintain strict confidentiality in all cases involving students' personal files. In cases involving a claim of personal injury, the burden of proof rests with the student in demonstrating that actual harm has occurred owing to the deliberate communication of sensitive information to a third party.

Libel

Libel, unlike slander, is written defamation. Teachers, counselors, and principals should refrain from including in the student's record damaging information for which there is no basis. Any information recorded should be factual and specific with respect to serious infractions committed by the student—for example, time and place when infractions occurred and possible witnesses who might verify, if needed, that the incident described is an accurate account of what actually occurred.

Another consideration involves a determination as to whether certain types of information should be included in the student's permanent file. Some legal experts feel that information that is subject to change and information about minor disciplinary infractions should be maintained in a separate file and destroyed after the student leaves school. For example, if there is no evidence of a serious and recurring behavior problem, one might question the wisdom of including a single occurrence on the student's permanent records. However, if there is a strong belief that the behavior is sufficiently serious that it needs to be passed on to those who will be working with the student in the future, it might be appropriate, under the circumstances, to retain such information permanently. Sound and rational judgment is required in these cases. These decisions must be carefully drawn, because of the serious implications involved. When it becomes necessary to record a serious disciplinary infraction on the student's record, the document should, if possible, be executed in the presence of the student, who should be provided a copy of the document.

School personnel should refrain from making statements that are based on opinion, particularly those involving questions of morality, contagious diseases, family marital conditions, and mental or emotional issues. These statements are damaging by their content and, if communicated to others, may result in injury to the student's reputation, self-esteem, or standing in the school. Statements that categorize or stereotype students should be avoided. If educators adhere to confidentiality and respect for the privacy rights of students, they will avoid liability claims of injury to students. Professionalism and ethics dictate that these practices be followed.

Privilege

On many occasions, school personnel are requested to provide either oral or written information regarding a student, some of which may be contained in the student's file. When such requests are made and school personnel respond in a truthful and reasonable manner in accordance with their prescribed duties, they are protected by qualified privilege. When school personnel and the recipient of the information both have a legitimate interest, they also are protected by a qualified privilege when the communication is reasonable to achieve their objective. Those who have a common interest would likely include counselors, subject matter teachers, administrators, and parents. Note that this privilege does not extend to one to whom communication subsequently is transmitted and who does not share this common interest and consequently has no need to be apprised of the information.

Good Faith

Qualified privilege is based on the premise that the educator is operating in good faith. *Good faith* requires that a legitimate purpose be served by communicating the information. Common interest in the student's well-being would constitute a legitimate purpose. Good faith efforts dictate that as information is shared with other eligible parties, it is communicated for legitimate purposes and without any intent or desire to damage the student. An absence of good faith may result in personal damages against those who do not operate in a reasonable and prudent manner.

Acts of Malice

Malice exists when there is intent to harm or injure another. Intent is an important element in malicious behavior. When statements are communicated regarding a student, either written or oral, with the intent to injure his or her reputation, a tortious act has occurred, especially if the statements are false. *Truth* is a defense against liability if no malicious intent is present. School personnel should exercise care in ensuring that statements communicated to others are free of malice; based on defensible evidence; and communicated in a professional, nonbiased, and truthful manner. When evidence reveals that school personnel acted in bad faith with the intent to injure a student's reputation and standing in the school or community, liability charges may be justified even if the statements are true. Students are entitled to the expectation that their reputation will be protected against unwarranted attacks.

There are essentially two types of malice. In *implied malice*, the offender has no excuse for conveying harmful information. Such information normally falls into the category of unsolicited or derogatory statements aimed at another person. In *actual malice*, the person offended must demonstrate that the person making the offensive comment had a motive for doing so and that this motive was calculated to generate ill will against the offended person. An accusation of either type may create serious legal problems for school personnel.

Educators should be mindful not to express opinions about students that might be damaging without having the factual information to validate their statements. Any statements regarding another's mental, psychological, or emotional status are very risky. These types of statements should be avoided. Educators should provide only reasonable information, based on good faith and about which they are qualified to provide. Even though truth is a defense against defamation claims, it is not absolute. If statements are made about another that will automatically result in injury to that person's reputation, truth will not be a reasonable defense in this situation. Statements, if true, involving marital status, sexual preference, or contagious diseases may result in defamation charges if persons against whom these statements are made can prove that they sustained damages.

CONFIDENTIALITY ISSUES INVOLVING SCHOOL COUNSELORS

A number of states have passed laws protecting the confidentiality of counselors. Most states do not support confidentiality protection for counselors. Michigan and Nevada have the most complete protection. South Dakota, Ohio, Maine, Oregon, Alabama, Arkansas, Idaho, Indiana, Kentucky, Missouri, Montana, North Carolina, Oregon, and Pennsylvania provide protection to counselors in civil and criminal proceedings. However, most communication between a school counselor and a student does not rise to become evidence in a civil or criminal proceeding. In states where no privilege is granted, the counselor is required to testify if ordered by the court.

In the school setting, counselors are not required to share information obtained from students with their parents. Records that remain in the sole possession of counselors are not subject to FERPA. That is, education records under

FERPA do not include personal files of counselors. Confidentiality, however, is not absolute. When circumstances arise in which disclosure is in the public interest, confidentiality is lost. One of the most significant examples is *Tarasoff v. Regents of the University of California* in 1976, in which a student confided to his psychologist during a therapy session that he was going to kill another student.[5] Tatiana Tarasoff was subsequently killed by the student. Her parents filed suit, claiming that the psychologist had a duty to warn their daughter and them of an impending danger. The psychologist did, however, inform campus police. The Supreme Court of California ruled that the psychologist had a duty to warn the victim. Further, the psychologist became sufficiently involved to assume some responsibility for the safety not only of the patient but also of any person whom the psychologist knew to be endangered by the patient.

GUIDES

Liability and Student Records

1. School districts and schools should have legally defensible policies and procedures consistent with the requirements of FERPA. Students, parents, and legal guardians should be informed of their rights under this act.
2. Accurate records should be maintained in the student's file, indicating the name, title, date, description of educational interest, specific records examined, and the place of examination of student records for those who have access.
3. Any corrections or adjustments to student records should be dated and initialed by the person responsible, with the knowledge and approval of school officials.
4. School personnel should avoid labeling children in ways that damage the student's self-esteem.
5. When it becomes necessary to place disciplinary infraction information on student records, the information should be specific regarding the infraction committed—time, place, and witnesses, as appropriate. The student should be present when this information is recorded.
6. Teachers should refrain from aimless chatter involving third parties, originating from confidential information found on student records. Gossip or careless talk among school personnel calculated to harm a student is not protected by qualified privilege.

7. Student records should be maintained in a safe and secure place and should not be removed from school premises by school personnel unless proper authorization is received.

8. Unless prohibited by court order, the noncustodial parent should be afforded the same right to access student records as the custodial parent.

9. Releasing information over the telephone should be avoided, unless the identity of the other party has been firmly established.

10. Public disclosures of students' grades will not likely be supported by the courts. Such practices violate the intent of FERPA and should not be supported by school officials.

PRACTICAL TIPS

Do:

1. Recognize the important role that teachers play in protecting students' confidential information. Failure to do so may lead to violations of students' right to privacy, which may leave teachers vulnerable to legal challenges by parents or legal guardians.

2. Make certain that any information recorded on student confidential records is specific, defensible, and within the guidelines established by the statute and school district policy. This step will minimize the potential for charges of defamation.

3. Review student records to ascertain pertinent information. This information will contribute to your ability to provide an effective learning experience for students.

4. Consult with the school principal or guidance counselor regarding any questionable information that should or should not be recorded on a student's confidential record. Consultation will ensure that inappropriate student information will not be retained in those records.

Do not:

1. Discuss any student's confidential information inappropriately or with individuals who have no need to know the information. Such disclosure violates a student's right to confidentiality.

2. Ignore the fact that teachers may be sued for defamation when they are found guilty of libel or slander

toward students. Libel and slander are valid grounds for lawsuits.

3. Include information on a student's record that is based on personal opinion. Only factual information is defensible to avoid challenges involving inaccuracies in a student's records.

4. Use malicious communication or an intent to harm a student's reputation or standing in school on the basis of conflicts with the student. Truth will not protect teachers from defamation when there is evidence of intentional malice directed toward a student.

5. Fail to meet the requirements of good faith when communicating student information to others. A legitimate defensible purpose must be served when information is disclosed to other authorized recipients.

ENDNOTES

1. 20 USC S. 1232 g.
2. 34 C. F. R. § 99.6
3. *Page v. Rotterdam-Mohonasen Central School District,* 441 N.Y.S.2d 323 (Sup. Ct. 1981).
4. *Owasso Independent School District No. 1-011 v. Falvo,* 534 U.S. 426; 122 S. Ct. 934; 151 L. Ed. 2d 896 (2002).
5. *Tarasoff v. Regents of the University of California,* 17 Cal.3d 425; 551 P.2d 334; 131 Cal. Rptr. 14 (1976).

7

Individuals with Disabilities

In 1975, Congress enacted P.L. 94-142, the Education for All Handicapped Children Act (EAHCA), based on findings that supported the need for it. Congress discerned that there were more than 8 million children in the United States with disabilities whose needs had not been fully met. Roughly 4 million of these same children had not been provided appropriate education services that would allow them to receive an equal educational opportunity. Even more startling was the realization that more than a million children with disabilities had not received any type of public educational opportunity. Many of those who did receive some form of public education were not able to receive the full benefits of an educational experience because their disabilities had not been diagnosed. In many instances, parents were forced to seek assistance for their children with disabilities outside the public school arena, often at great expense and inconvenience to the family.

On the basis of these findings, Congress realized that it was in the nation's best interest for the federal government to intervene and work collaboratively with states in addressing the needs of children with disabilities throughout the country. This intervention was presented in the form of P.L. 94-142. EAHCA has undergone a number of amendments since its inception. As of 1990, it has been referred to as the *Individuals with Disabilities Education Act (IDEA)*. Although the act has been amended on a number of occasions—most recently in 2004—and renamed the Individuals with Disability Education Improvement Act (IDEIA), its primary purpose has remained intact.

There has been a steady increase in the number of children classified with disabilities. This growth trend highlights the importance of the efforts to continue to improve services to meet the educational needs of these children and provide equal access to educational opportunities.

Individuals with disabilities are protected by three significant federal statutes: IDEIA) of 2004; the Americans with Disabilities Act (ADA) of 1990, amended in 2008; and the Rehabilitation Act of 1973, Section 504. These statutes were enacted to protect individuals with disabilities from discrimination and provide them equal access to educational opportunities, facility utilization, and employment opportunities in public school settings. The ADA Amendments Act of 2008 made important changes to the definition of the term *disability*. The amended act took effect January 1, 2009. (See a summary of significant changes in Chapter 9.)

INDIVIDUALS WITH DISABILITIES EDUCATION IMPROVEMENT ACT OF 2004 (IDEIA)

Mandatory Requirements

As stated previously, IDEA and, subsequently, IDEIA succeeded EAHCA. Congress passed IDEA to clearly define the responsibilities of school districts regarding children with disabilities and to provide a measure of financial support to assist states in meeting their obligations. IDEA covers infants and toddlers from birth to age 2, and their families, with early intervention services.

Additionally, IDEA essentially guarantees children with disabilities, ages 3 to 21, the right to a free, appropriate education in public schools. The act also establishes substantive and procedural due process rights for disabled students. To meet eligibility requirements, a state must develop a plan to ensure a free, appropriate education for all children with disabilities within its jurisdiction. In addition, each state must formulate a policy that ensures certain due process rights for all children with disabilities. The state plan should include its goals and a timetable for meeting these goals, as well as the personnel, facilities, and related services necessary to meet the needs of children with disabilities. The state plan also must include a well-designed system for allocating funds to local school districts. In turn, each local district must submit an application to the state demonstrating how it will comply with the requirements of IDEA. District plans must be on file and available for review by citizens, on request.

IDEA requires each state to allocate federal funds first to children with disabilities who are not receiving any type of education and subsequently to children with the most severe disabilities within each disability category. IDEA further stipulates that, to the fullest extent possible, children with disabilities must be educated with children having no disabilities. In principle, no child with disabilities may be excluded from receiving a free, appropriate public education. The statute does not require disabled children to demonstrate, as a condition of receiving public education services, that they will benefit from special education. Because there is such a wide array of disabilities, IDEA does not require equality of results; it merely requires that children with disabilities benefit from instruction.

Functional Exclusion of Children with Disabilities

Two practices tend to create additional challenges for children with disabilities: exclusion from educational programs and misclassification based on improper assessment. Both practices may result in functional exclusion of children with disabilities. *Functional exclusion* occurs when children with disabilities receive a highly inappropriate placement that denies them an opportunity to receive an appropriate education. Both practices will generally result in legal challenges. In recent years, because of IDEA, considerable progress has been made regarding the inclusion of students with disabilities. Unfortunately, errors continue to occur regarding proper classification and placement. Consequently, school officials should exercise caution to ensure that classification and placement of children with disabilities is implemented properly.

Interpretation and Identification of Children with Disabilities

The term *children with disabilities* is defined by IDEA as those who meet the following conditions:

> *Mental retardation, hearing impairments which include deafness, speech or language impairment, visual impairment including blindness, learning disabilities, brain injury, emotional disturbance, orthopedic impairments, autism, traumatic brain injury, specific learning disabilities and other impairments who by reason of such conditions need special education and related services.*[1]

Response to Intervention

Regular classroom teachers have the responsibility for identifying students who may need special services to receive the full benefits of an education. Response to Intervention (RtI) is a method of academic intervention used to provide early, effective assistance to children who are experiencing difficulty learning. According to the National Center for Response Intervention, "Data-based decision making is the essence of good RTI practice; it is essential for the other three components, screening: progress monitoring and multi-leveled instruction. All components must be implemented using culturally responsive and evidence based practices."[2] The method requires children to demonstrate a notable inconsistency between their IQ and academic achievement as determined by standardized tests. RtI more clearly defines the Specific Learning Disability (SLD) category of IDEIA. Students who do not respond to effective interventions are more likely to experience learning difficulties that require special education.

After the regular classroom teacher has worked with a student and is convinced that the student needs special assistance, the teacher makes a request in the form of a *referral*. Virtually all school districts have well-developed policies and procedures regarding referrals. Although these procedures vary from district to district, usually there is some type of referral form used by the regular teacher when a student is deemed to need special services. This form should be as inclusive as possible in providing the relevant information needed to conduct a formal assessment of the student if such an assessment is required. Data requested on the referral form may include the student's name; present grade level and age; gender; standardized test scores; local test data; strengths and weaknesses in key subject areas; reading ability; behavior and relationships with fellow students; pertinent family data; and teaching methods or strategies that have been successful, as well as those that have been unsuccessful.

If a formal assessment procedure is contemplated, the student's parent or legal guardian must grant consent and be informed of the student's personal rights under due process provisions. Teachers should approach the referral process with great care, because it influences the student's education, consumes time and district resources, and may result in stigmatizing a student. It is not uncommon for districts to hold prereferral conferences to discuss concerns regarding the student's academic and social performance. These meetings usually involve the referring teacher, a special education professional, the principal, the counselor, and, in many instances, the parent or legal guardian. Such meetings may be used as an intermediate measure to discuss the implementation of new and different strategies to enhance the student's academic and social performance. During this time, an evaluation period should be established to assess the student's progress before a formal assessment is contemplated and decisions are made regarding the need for special services. It is highly desirable to employ some type of intervention prior to implementing a formal assessment process. This measure, if implemented appropriately, may reduce overreferrals and misclassifications and should result in the best education program for the student, particularly when new strategies and interventions are implemented and evaluated over a reasonable length of time. The school's review process should be consistent with state and federal regulations. If it is determined that the student's problem stems from a disability, a classification is agreed on during the conference in which the parent or legal guardian is present. Once the classification is agreed on, this information is passed on to a committee, who, along with the parent, engages in developing the student's individualized educational program (IEP). The parent must sign the IEP and approve any placement outside the regular classroom.

School districts are required to evaluate every child with disabilities to determine the nature of the disability and the need for special education and related services. Prior to this evaluation, each district must forward to the child's parent a written notice, in the parent's native language, describing the proposed evaluation process. Parental consent must be sought prior to the actual evaluation. If consent is not obtained, the district must initiate an impartial hearing through a hearing officer to secure approval to conduct the evaluation in the absence of parental consent.

Once approval is granted, the evaluation must be fully objective and free of any form of bias. It should be conducted in the child's native language by a multidisciplinary team qualified to assess a wide range of skill areas. Every effort must be made to ensure that only validated tests designed to assess specific areas of need are utilized. This evaluation process should occur in a timely fashion and address each area of the child's suspected disability.

No single test should be used as the sole criterion for determining disabilities but, rather, a battery of appropriate tests designed to assess areas of suspected disabilities should be administered. The child's strengths and weaknesses should be identified during this process, as these will determine, to a large extent, the nature of his or her individualized program. A parent or legal guardian who is dissatisfied with the evaluation may secure an independent evaluation at the school district's expense, unless the hearing officer agrees with the district's assessment. In either case, each child with disabilities should be reevaluated, at a minimum, every 3 years, unless the parents and district agree that a reevaluation is unnecessary. RiT may be utilized by school districts for all students who are experiencing difficulty in achieving desired learning outcomes. It may also be used as a transformational model to enhance and sustain student achievement at all levels. RiT provides a high level of accountability for school leaders, teachers, and students.

Individualized Education Program (IEP) Requirement

When the evaluation results are produced, an IEP must be designed for each child with disabilities. This process usually involves one or more meetings in which the child's teacher, parent or legal guardian, and special education representative for the district are present to review and discuss evaluation results. It is also recommended that a representative from the evaluation team be present to respond to questions and to interpret results. If feasible, this representative may be the child's teacher or the special education supervisor. At a minimum, each IEP should include the following:

1. a statement detailing the child's present level of educational performance;
2. a statement of annual goals, as well as short-term instructional objectives;
3. a description of specific education services to be provided and a determination as to whether the child is able to participate in regular educational programs;
4. a description of transition services to be rendered if the child is a junior or senior in high school, to ensure that necessary services are provided when the child leaves the regular school environment;
5. a description of services to be provided and a timetable for providing these services;
6. an explanation of relevant criteria and procedures to be employed annually to determine whether instructional objectives have been achieved; and
7. an annual review of the student's IEP, and recommended modifications as needed.

No Child Left Behind

The task force on No Child Left Behind (NCLB), in its final report, made a number of recommendations regarding students with disabilities, to provide increased flexibility to states. In its report, the task force

1. urged Congress to recognize the IDEIA as the prevailing law that should take precedence over NCLB. Thus, states should be allowed to use IEPs to determine appropriate curriculum standards and tests;
2. proposed that states should be allowed to determine the percentage of special education populations that would best be educated according to out-of-level standards and tested accordingly, on the basis of IEPs; and
3. advocated that the U.S. Department of Education publicize to states the option of setting a different minimum on the number of students needed to establish a subgroup in school, for reporting purposes.

Least Restrictive Environment

IDEA embraces the notion that children with disabilities should be placed in educational settings that offer the least number of restrictions, when appropriate. This view is supported by the philosophy that children with disabilities, to the greatest degree possible, should be educated with children having no disabilities, under normal classroom conditions. The primary objective is to provide the child with disabilities an opportunity to interact, socialize, and learn with regular students, thus minimizing the tendency of the child to become stigmatized and isolated from the school's regular program. There is also inherent value in providing students without disabilities an opportunity to increase their awareness of, and to be sensitized to, the many challenges faced by children with disabilities. Therefore, the least restrictive provision of the act mandates the inclusion of students with disabilities into regular classrooms.

This regulation is designed to ensure that students with disabilities be provided the broadest range of opportunities and is based on the least restrictive environment (LRE) provisions. The interpretation of precisely what constitutes the least restrictive environment has led to conflicts as well as litigation. Generally, when a child with disabilities is not involved in regular classroom instruction, the district must demonstrate through the evaluation and IEP process that a segregated facility would represent a more appropriate and beneficial learning environment for that child. Because the law indicates a strong preference for inclusion, the burden of proof rests with educators to demonstrate that their decisions are not arbitrary or capricious regarding the placement of children with disabilities. The statute does not mandate inclusion in each case but does require that it be used to the fullest extent possible and as appropriate, according to the unique needs of the child with disabilities.

LRE is a relative concept. What constitutes the LRE for one child might be totally inappropriate for another. Because there is such wide variation of needs among students with disabilities, there is no ideal way to provide appropriate education services to such children. Given the variations among these students, a range of placement options must be provided. These options might include, but are not limited to, the following possibilities:

- regular class with support from regular classroom teachers,
- regular class with support instruction from special teachers,
- regular class with special resource instruction,
- full-time special education class in regular school,
- full-time special school,
- residential school, and
- homebound instruction.

The particular placement options should be determined by the needs of the child who has disabilities and the type of environment that will best meet his or her educational and social needs.

Under the concept of inclusion, regular classroom teachers in schools across the country are challenged to meet the needs of students with disabilities. In many instances, they are unprepared to do so. Because IDEA specifies that students with disabilities be provided a free, appropriate public education in the LRE, according to the student's IEP, there is an affirmative obligation placed on schools to serve the needs of students with disabilities. If teachers are not prepared to meet these needs, a legal issue may emerge regarding academic, emotional, and physical injury to the student with disabilities.

Regular classroom teachers are called on, with increasing frequency, to meet the academic needs and perform health-related services such as catheterization, suctioning, stoma care, and seizure monitoring when students with disabilities are placed in regular classrooms. If teachers are unable to perform these vital services effectively and their failure results in injury to the child with disabilities, liability charges may be forthcoming, depending on the nature of the injury and factors leading to such injury. Therefore, such classroom teachers must be fully trained to meet the academic needs of children with disabilities and, in most cases, provide special education services during the inclusion period.

Equal Access to Assistive Technology for Students with Disabilities

The Technology-Related Assistance for Individuals with Disabilities Act Amendment of 1994 provides financial assistance to states to support systems changes intended to assist in the development and implementation of technology-related support for individuals with disabilities. The amended act further ensures timely acquisition and delivery of assistive technology devices, including equipment and product systems commercially acquired, modified, or customized that are used to increase, maintain, or improve functional capabilities of a child with disabilities, but not including surgically implanted medical devices.

Technology assistive services are also included in this act and involve any service that directly assists a child with a disability in the selection, acquisition, or use of an assistive technology device. These services may include (a) purchasing, leasing, or otherwise providing for the acquisition of assistive technology by the child with disabilities; (b) selecting, designing, fitting, customizing, adapting, applying, maintaining, repairing, or replacing assistive technology devices; (c) coordinating and using other therapies, interventions, or services with assistive technology devices such as those associated with existing education and rehabilitation plans and programs; (d) training or technical assistance for the child with disabilities or, where appropriate, the family of such child; and (e) training or technical assistance for professionals (including individuals providing education and rehabilitation services), employers, and other individuals who provide services to, or otherwise substantially participate in, the major life functions of such child.

Program Review and Changes

As previously stated, each IEP must be reviewed and revised annually, if necessary, to ensure that the continuing needs of the child are met. However, under the 2004 reauthorization, the secretary of education is authorized to approve proposals for up to 15 states to allow school districts to develop a multi-year IEP for a maximum of 3 years, with parental consent. The IEP is not necessarily reviewed annually. When changes are contemplated, the child's parent or legal guardian must be notified. If the parent or legal guardian objects to the proposed changes, an impartial hearing must be held to resolve the conflict. If this process proves unsuccessful, the parent or guardian may appeal to the state agency and, subsequently, to the courts if a resolution is not reached at the state level. This appeals process is designed to ensure fundamental fairness and to meet the requirements of due process, as spelled out in IDEIA.

Education-Related Service Requirement

A *related service* is a service that must be provided to allow the child with disabilities to benefit from special education. A related service may be a single service or an entire range of services or programs needed to benefit the child. Examples of such services include, but are not limited to, the following: transportation, medical services, counseling services, psychological services, physical therapy, speech pathology, audiology, occupational therapy, and specific medical services.

Inclusion of Children with Disabilities

Inclusion is an extension of the traditional concept of *mainstreaming*. Its intent is to ensure, as much as possible and when appropriate, that children with disabilities be placed in regular classrooms. Inclusion is one mechanism designed to ensure that children with disabilities receive a free, appropriate education in an effort to maximize their learning potential.

Implicit in this concept is the view that some educational benefit is conferred on students with disabilities when they attend public schools. A child's evaluation results, which are used to develop the IEP, ultimately determine the nature of the placement. Because the IEP is tailored specifically to meet the needs of the child with disabilities, it must be reasonably calculated to enable the child to receive the benefit of instruction.

Inclusion also is valuable in integrating children with disabilities into the regular school program. Many educators feel that both groups of children—those with and those without disabilities—benefit from this arrangement. Although numerous educators support inclusion as one design that places children with disabilities in the most ideal educational environment, many others feel that inclusion places these children in nonsupportive environments, taking away valuable time from their learning activities, particularly in environments where the classroom teacher is not properly trained to work with children who have disabilities. The preparation of teachers to meet the needs of these children is critical, because inclusion is an important component of IDEA, which supports equal access for children with disabilities.

Attention Deficit Hyperactivity Disorder and Federal Protection

A growing number of children with attention deficit hyperactivity disorder (ADHD) are enrolled in public schools. Three federal statutes—IDEIA (2004), Section 504 of the Rehabilitation Act (1973), and ADA—cover children with ADHD.

Under IDEIA, ADHD-eligible students must possess one or more specified physical or mental impairments and must have been determined to require special education and related services on the basis of these impairments. ADHD alone is not sufficient to qualify a child for special education services, unless the condition impairs the child's ability to benefit from education. Children with ADHD may be eligible for special education services if they are found to have a specific learning disability, to be seriously emotionally disturbed, or to possess other health impairments.

DISCIPLINING STUDENTS WITH DISABILITIES

It has long been held that children with disabilities may not be punished for conduct that is a *manifestation* of their disability. However, school personnel may discipline students with disabilities for any behavior that is not associated with their disability, as long as regular disciplinary procedures as reflected in school policies, are used. When certain types of discipline are warranted, an effort must be made to ensure that the punishment does not *materially* and *substantially* interrupt the child's education. School suspensions, transfers, and expulsion are examples that fall into this category.

Expulsion

Children with disabilities are neither immune from a school's disciplinary process nor entitled to participate in programs when their behavior impairs the education of other children in the program. School officials may exercise at least two options in this situation. First, school authorities may take swift disciplinary measures, such as suspension, against disruptive children with disabilities. Second, a planning and placement team (PPT) may request a change in placement to a more restrictive environment for children with disabilities who have demonstrated, by disrupting the education of other children, that their present placement is inappropriate. IDEIA thereby affords schools with both short- and long-term methods for dealing with children with disabilities who present behavioral problems.

Schools may use their normal disciplinary procedures to address the behavior of students with disabilities if that behavior is not disability related. As ruled in the 1981 case *S-1 v. Turlington*, school authorities may not discipline students with disabilities for behavior that is a manifestation of their disability.[3] Because certain types of disciplinary measures may involve removal of children with disabilities from their placement, caution must be exercised to ensure that proper procedural guidelines are followed. As established in an early case, *Stuart v. Nappi* in 1978, suspension of a student with disabilities is tantamount to a change in placement, thus triggering the "stay put" provision of IDEIA.[4] These decisions may involve transfers, suspensions, and expulsions. The "stay put" provision of IDEIA requires that children with disabilities remain in their current placement, pending the completion of the IEP review process.

When there is agreement between the parent and school authorities, the child remains in the current placement, even though it may not be deemed the most appropriate one at that time.[5] If either the parent or school authorities wish to temporarily change the placement before the appeals process is exhausted, a court order must be obtained to effect this change. If a decision is reached that a child's placement should be changed, special education and related services cannot be discontinued. The child must receive education support.

Suspension

School suspension is one of the most common forms of punishment used to remove disruptive students from the school environment. It is particularly useful as a disciplinary tool when there is an immediate threat to the health and safety of the child with disabilities or of other children in the school. A temporary suspension may be justified in cases that fall into this category. There has been considerable disagreement among school officials regarding the limits of their authority to temporarily remove children with disabilities in emergency situations when the health and safety of students are threatened.

In a compelling 1988 case, *Honig v. Doe*, the U.S. Supreme Court responded to this issue. This case involved two emotionally disturbed students who had been suspended indefinitely for violent conduct related to their disabilities, pending the results of an expulsion hearing. Both students filed suit, contending that the suspensions and proposed expulsions violated the "stay put" provision of IDEIA. The district court ruled for the students, and the decision was later affirmed by the court of appeals. The case was then reviewed by the U.S. Supreme Court. The fundamental issue confronting the High Court was whether the "stay put" provision of IDEIA prohibits states from removing children with disabilities from school for violent or disruptive conduct stemming from their disability. The High Court ruled that, under the act, states shall not remove students with disabilities from classrooms for violent or disruptive conduct stemming from their disability.

Schools, however, may use their normal procedures in dealing with students who endanger themselves or others. Students who pose an immediate threat to school safety may be temporarily suspended for up to 10 days without any inquiry into whether the student's behavior was a manifestation of a disability. This type of suspension—consistent with an earlier case in 1975, *Goss v. Lopez*, involving students without disabilities—is considered to be a short-term measure that allows school authorities the freedom to discipline a student with disabilities by removing the student from the classroom in anticipation of further action, which may involve long-term suspension, movement to a more restrictive environment, or, as a last resort, expulsion.[6]

The significance of this ruling is that the High Court did not interpret short-term suspension as a change in placement and therefore did not hold that such discipline triggers the need for elaborate procedural requirements associated with IDEIA.[7] However, it is important to note that long-term suspensions and expulsions do constitute a change in placement and may not be used if the student's conduct is associated with a known disability. Under the 1997 amendments to IDEA regarding discipline, a student may be placed in an Interim Alternative Education Setting (IAES) for up to 45 days, provided, however, that the same sanction is used for students without disabilities. This sanction applies if the student carries a weapon to school or a school function, or illegally uses drugs, or sells or solicits the sale of a controlled substance, at school or a school function. (For weapons and/or drugs discipline, "stay put" does not apply.)

Congress approved the reauthorized IDEIA, and President George W. Bush signed the act into law. Most provisions of the act were effective July 5, 2005. The following tables summarize the major changes under the new reauthorization act.

TABLE 7.1 Summary of Significant Changes to the IDEIA Reauthorization Act of 2004

1997	2004
Teacher Qualifications	**Teacher Qualifications**
Special education teachers do not fall under NCLB's definition of a highly qualified teacher.	All special education teachers fall under NCLB definition and must possess a special education certificate or pass a state licensing exam; must not have had a waiver on an emergency, temporary, or provisional basis; and must have earned a bachelor's degree.
Funds	**Funds**
Funding formula does not include per-pupil expenditures in the United States based on such expenditures during the current fiscal year.	Funds allocated to state and local education agencies for special education and related services are based on average per-pupil expenditures in the United States during the current fiscal year.
Eligibility Determination	**Eligibility Determination**
Timeline for parental consent for determination of eligibility is not established.	A 60-day timeline is established from receipt of parental consent for evaluation regarding a determination of eligibility to meeting the educational needs of the child.
Transition Services	**Transition Services**
Transition services do not specify age of children with disabilities.	Transition services are required when the child with disabilities reaches age 16.
Individual Education Program	**Individual Education Program**
School personnel in all school districts are required to review and revise the IEP annually. Short-term objectives are required of all children with disabilities, as a component of the IEP.	

(continued)

**TABLE 7.1   Summary of Significant Changes
to the IDEIA Reauthorization Act of 2004 (*continued*)**

1997	2004
Multiyear IEP	**Multiyear IEP**
The secretary of education is authorized to approve proposals for up to 15 states to allow school districts to develop a multiyear IEP for a maximum of 3 years with parental consent. The IEP will not necessarily be reviewed annually. Short-term objectives are no longer required, except for children who are meeting alternative assessment requirements and/or students with the most significant cognitive disabilities.	Participating states must meet the following criteria: States must agree to participate in a quasi-experimental research evaluation design study using data on educational and functional results for students with disabilities, submit time allocated and resource expenditures by IEP team members and teachers, and assess the quality of long-term education plans incorporated in IEPs. LEAs must agree to fully cooperate in the evaluation process and provide all required information and data including access to multiyear IEPs and nonmultiyear IEPs from matched participating children with disabilities. States must describe how the state obtained broad stakeholder input (from school and district personnel and parents) in developing the list of required elements for each multiyear IEP and the process for the review and revision of each multiyear IEP. States must ensure that parents are informed in writing of any differences between the requirements relating to the content, development, review, and revision of IEPs. If changes are contemplated, the child's parent or legal guardian must be notified.

TABLE 7.1 (*continued*)

1997	2004
Related Services	**Related Services**
Provisions of the IEP do not require that comparable related services be provided to a child with disabilities who transfers to another school district within the state during the same school year. Examples of related services include transportation, medical services, counseling services, psychological services, physical therapy, speech pathology, audiology, and occupational therapy.	Comparable related services must be provided to a child with disabilities who transfers to a new school district within his or her state during the same school year. Services are expanded to include nursing and interpreting services.
Manifestation	**Manifestation**
The burden of proof rests with schools to demonstrate that behavior resulting in disciplinary action is not a manifestation of the child's disability.	The burden now shifts from schools to parents, who must demonstrate that the child's behavior is substantially related to his or her disability.
Placement	**Placement**
Limited discretion is given to schools to determine placement for children with disabilities who violate a student code of conduct.	School personnel may consider, on a case-by-case basis, the unique circumstances when deciding whether to prescribe a change in placement for a child with disabilities who violates a code of conduct.
Attorneys' Fees	**Attorneys' Fees**
Attorneys' fees are awarded to parents who file a substantive complaint regarding their rights or the rights of their child with a disability.	A state or local educational agency may be awarded attorneys' fees if it prevails in court in cases of frivolous or unreasonable complaints by parents or the pursuit of a frivolous complaint by attorneys.
Stay Put	**Stay Put**
Students with disabilities are permitted to remain in their current placement, pending appeal, in cases regarding violations involving drugs, weapons, or other dangerous activity.	A stay put provision is eliminated for alleged violations of a school code that may result in a removal from a student's current education placement for more than 10 days.

(*continued*)

**TABLE 7.1 Summary of Significant Changes
to the IDEIA Reauthorization Act of 2004 (*continued*)**

1997	2004
IEP Team Attendance	**IEP Team Attendance**
All IEP team members are required to attend the annual program review meeting.	A member of the IEP team shall not be required to attend all or part of the IEP meeting if the parent (in writing) and the LEA agree that the team member's attendance is not necessary because the member's area of curriculum or related service is not being modified or discussed during the meeting.
IEP Meeting	**IEP Meeting**
If changes to a child's IEP are necessary after the annual IEP meeting, the IEP committee is required to meet to amend the current IEP.	If changes to the IEP are necessary after the annual meeting for the school year, the parent and the LEA may agree not to convene an IEP meeting to make the changes but, instead, develop a written document to amend or modify the current IEP.
Learning Disabilities	**Learning Disabilities**
A battery of appropriate tests is used during the evaluation process to determine whether a child has a disability.	Local educational agencies may use an evaluation process to determine whether a child responds to scientific research–based intervention as a part of the required evaluation procedures used when addressing specific learning disabilities.
Testing	**Testing**
There is limited flexibility to use alternative assessments.	States are provided the option of testing up to 2% of their students by using alternative assessment based on modified standards.
Mandatory Requirements	**Mandatory Requirements**
Mandatory services do not address graduation rates, dropout rates, or other relevant factors, as determined by states.	Each state must establish goals that address graduation rates and dropout rates, as well as other factors each state may determine.

Rehabilitation Act of 1973, Section 504

Public school students with certain disabilities that are not covered under IDEIA may be covered under Section 504 of the Rehabilitation Act of 1973. For example, students with ADHD may receive special education services if there is evidence that they have a learning disability or any other type of impairment that adversely affects their ability to capitalize on an equal education opportunity. Students who are covered by Section 504 may receive regular or special education and related services that allow them to receive an appropriate education after they are evaluated and placed according to documented needs. The assessment process is not as extensive as the process related to IDEIA, but the objectives are very similar. Section 504 requires that

- assessment or evaluation of students with special needs be conducted;
- parents be provided a right to contest evaluation results;
- the school district develop an IEP for either regular or special education related services;
- the child receive an education in a regular class setting, unless it is determined that regular instruction, along with supplemental aids, is insufficient to achieve satisfactory results; and
- teachers make necessary adjustments in regular classroom instruction to meet the educational needs of students who are covered under the Rehabilitation Act.

GUIDES

Students with Disabilities

1. School districts should ensure that children with disabilities in their districts be provided equal access to a public education. Failure to provide appropriate special education may result in a court injunction, as well as in mandatory compensatory education.
2. A well-organized and coordinated staff development plan should be developed to prepare all teachers to work effectively with children who have disabilities. These activities should be coherent, continuous, and well supported by the district.
3. School personnel should be aware of potential liability challenges if they fail to perform certain related services properly.

4. Parental rights must be respected and addressed in matters relating to evaluation and IEP development.

5. Children with disabilities should not be disciplined for behavior that is associated with their known disability.

6. Long-term suspension, if necessary, will trigger the need for change of placement requirements, but in virtually no cases should children with disabilities be without education services. School officials should become familiar with the new IDEA amendments regarding discipline of students with disabilities and be certain that the standards are incorporated into district policy.

7. The burden of proof rests with parents in demonstrating that a student's misbehavior is substantially related to a disability.

8. According to one court, school districts are expected to provide sign language interpreters at district expense to deaf parents of hearing children at school-initiated activities related to the academic or disciplinary aspects of the child's education.

9. School districts may be required to provide education services beyond the regular school year, depending on the unique needs of the student with disabilities.

PRACTICAL TIPS

Do:

1. Understand that students with disabilities are entitled to the same educational opportunities as students without disabilities. Disabled students are protected by federal law and must receive a program of education and training commensurate with the student's capacity to learn.

2. Understand that all teachers should be prepared to teach students with disabilities whose IEP calls for inclusion. Inclusion in many instances allows disabled students to maximize their educational experiences.

3. Understand that all teachers have a responsibility to observe and identify students in their classes who might need special services to succeed in school. Various interventions and assessments should be conducted regarding learning difficulties, social and behavioral needs, and achievement deficiencies over a reasonable period.

4. Follow prescribed procedures to refer a student for an evaluation to determine whether special services are

needed. All relevant information should be provided regarding your efforts in working with the student academically and socially. This information will be needed to execute a formal evaluation if necessary.

Do not:

1. Discipline a child with disabilities unless you are certain that the unacceptable behavior is not associated with his or her disability. To do so would violate not only IDEIA but also the personal rights of the student with disabilities.
2. Do not isolate a student with disabilities unless authorized by school or district policy. Any form of isolation must be humane, safe, and not excessive for the student.
3. Fail to use positive behavior interventions and strategies to enhance learning opportunities for students with special needs. Positive behavior interventions may prevent harmful effects on students with special needs as well as other students in the classroom.

ENDNOTES

1. 20 U.S.C. § 1400 (C) (1988).
2. National Center for Response to Intervention, http://www.rti4success.org/.
3. *S-1 v. Turlington,* 635 F.2d 343 (5th Cir. Unit B Jan), *cert. denied,* 454 U.S. 1030 (1981).
4. *Stuart v. Nappi,* 443, F. Supp. 1235 (D. Conn. 1978).
5. 20 U.S.C. § 1415 (1997).
6. *Goss v. Lopez,* 419 U.S. 565, 95 S. Ct. 729, 42 L. Ed. 2d 725 (1975).
7. *Honig v. Doe,* 484 U.S. 305, 108 S. Ct. 592 (1988).

8

The Teacher and School Liability

School districts, school officials, and teachers may incur liability for their tortious acts when these acts result in injury to students. A *tort* is an actionable or civil wrong committed against one person by another that is independent of contract. If injury occurs as a result of the actions of school personnel, liability charges may be imminent. Liability may result from deliberate acts committed by another or acts involving negligence.

Students who are injured by school district personnel may claim monetary damages for their injury resulting from either intentional or unintentional torts. Under certain conditions, they also may seek injunctive relief to prevent the continuation of a harmful practice. Tort law further provides an opportunity for injured parties to bring charges when facts reveal that their reputation was injured.

In school settings, a tort may involve a class action suit affecting a number of school personnel, especially in cases involving negligent behavior. A tort may also involve actions brought against a single teacher, principal, or board member, depending on the circumstances surrounding the injury and the severity of the injury.

THE SCHOOL AS A SAFE PLACE

Schools are presumed to be safe places where teachers teach and students learn. The prevailing view held by the courts is that prudent professional educators, acting in place of parents, are supervising students under their care and ensuring, to the greatest extent possible, that they are safe. This doctrine is designed to provide parents reasonable assurance that their children are safe while under the supervision of responsible professional educators.

The doctrine places an affirmative obligation on all certified school personnel to take necessary measures to ensure that the school environment is safe for students and conducive to learning. In fact, teachers have been assigned three legal duties by the courts under *in loco parentis* (in place of parents): to instruct, supervise, and provide for the safety of students. Although there is little expectation that students will never be injured, there is an expectation that school personnel will exercise proper care to ensure, to the greatest extent possible, that students are protected from harm. When an unavoidable injury occurs, there is generally no liability. However, when injury is based on negligence, there are grounds for liability charges. In accordance with their legal duty, teachers are expected to foresee that students may be injured under certain circumstances. Once foreseeability is established, reasonable and necessary steps must be taken to prevent injury. In liability cases, courts will seek to determine whether school personnel knew or should have known of an impending danger and whether appropriate steps were taken to protect students. Simply stated, there is no defense for failure to take reasonable steps to prevent foreseeable harm to students in school.

LIABILITY OF SCHOOL PERSONNEL

School personnel are responsible for their own tortious acts in the school environment. Liability involving school personnel normally falls into two categories—intentional and unintentional torts. *Intentional torts* such as assault, battery, libel, slander, defamation (see the discussion of defamation in Chapter 6), false arrest, malicious prosecution, and invasion of privacy, require proof of intent or willfulness, whereas simple negligence, such as an *unintentional tort*, does not require such proof of intent or willfulness. In each case, liability charges may be sustained if the facts reveal that school personnel acted improperly or failed to act appropriately in situations involving students.

Individual Liability

In certain situations, school personnel may be held individually liable for their actions that result in injury to a student. Individual liability usually will not occur unless the plaintiff can demonstrate that a school employee's action violated a clearly established law and that the employee exhibited a reckless disregard for the rights of the plaintiff.[1]

The U.S. Supreme Court held in *Davis v. Scherer* that officials "are shielded from liability for civil damages if their conduct does not violate clearly established statutory or constitutional rights of which a reasonable person would have known" at the time of the incident.[2]

Vicarious Liability

Since school districts are employers of teachers, they also may be held vicariously liable for the negligent behavior of their employees. Under the historical theory of *respondeat superior*, the master is responsible only for authorized acts of its servants or agents. As applied in vicarious liability, the board rather than the principal is held liable for the tortious acts of its teachers, even though the board is not at fault. There is a requirement, under vicarious liability, that the teacher is acting within the scope of his or her assigned duties. This concept is most prevalent in cases involving negligence in which class action suits are brought against not only the teacher but also the school district for alleged negligence by the teacher.

Foreseeability

Foreseeability is a crucial element in liability cases, especially in cases involving negligence. *Foreseeability* is defined as the teacher's or administrator's ability to predict or anticipate that a certain activity or situation may prove harmful to students. Once this determination is made, there is an expectation that prudent steps will be taken to prevent harm to students. Failure to act in a prudent manner may result in liability claims. For example, a teacher could be held negligent when he or she leaves the classroom for an extended time and a student is injured during this absence. If the facts reveal that the students were immature and had a tendency to misbehave, and that the teacher's absence was unauthorized, it is foreseeable that an injury might occur. Whether an injury is foreseeable is a question of fact that will be determined by a jury in deciding whether liability should be imposed.

There are many instances when teachers and administrators are expected to foresee the potential danger associated with an activity or condition in the school. For example, if teachers or administrators observe broken glass panes in entry doors or in classrooms, it is foreseeable that a student entering the building or the room might sustain an injury if he or she makes contact with the broken glass panes. In this instance, schoolteachers and administrators have an obligation to warn students of the impending danger and to ensure that they are not injured. School personnel should report the broken panes to the proper authority so that they can be repaired promptly.

Similar expectations would apply in situations involving defective playground equipment, loose stair rails, or other nuisances (unsafe conditions) present in the school environment.

Nuisance

A *nuisance* may be described as any dangerous or hazardous condition that limits the free use of property by the user. The existence of such a condition in a school may require school personnel to exercise extra care to ensure that students are protected from possible harm. The implication suggested here is that school districts have an obligation to maintain safe premises for students under their supervision. School district personnel have the responsibility to inform students of unsafe conditions and to counsel students to stay away from dangerous situations, as well as to take reasonable measures to remove or correct hazardous conditions as soon as they become known.

In some instances, the question of attractive nuisance arises. An *attractive nuisance* is a dangerous instrument or condition that has a special attraction to a less mature child who does not appreciate the potential danger and who could be harmed. The standard of care increases in attractive nuisance cases.

An attractive nuisance claim will be supported if the evidence suggests one or more of the following:

1. Those responsible for the property knew or should have known that children would be attracted to the hazardous condition.
2. The responsible party knew that the hazardous condition posed an unreasonable risk to children.
3. Children, because of their youth, were unaware of the risk.
4. The utility to the owner of maintaining the risk and the cost of eliminating it were slight, as compared with the risk to children.
5. The owner failed to exercise reasonable care in eliminating the risk.[3]

Negligence claims may be supported if the evidence reveals that school personnel should have been aware of the hazard and were not diligent in responding to it. According to one court, however, it is unreasonable to expect that school personnel be required to discover or instantly correct every defect that is not of their own creation.[4] Reasonable action is required in cases involving nuisances. The courts have not required school personnel to ensure that all premises are perfectly safe at all times. If reasonable measures are taken, such as routine and periodic inspections and equipment repairs, then unanticipated or unexplained accidents usually will not generate liability charges against school personnel.

Because of their duty, teachers and administrators have a higher *standard of care* and are expected to *foresee* an accident more readily than would the average person. One of the fundamental questions raised by the courts in a case involving injury to a student is whether the teacher or administrator knew or should have known of the potential for harm to students. After an examination of facts, if the judge or jury determines that either teachers or administrators should have known of the impending danger and failed to act appropriately, liability charges will likely be imposed.

INTENTIONAL TORTS

As mentioned earlier, torts fall into two categories: intentional and unintentional. An intentional tort results from a *deliberate act* committed against another person. It may or may not be accompanied by malice. When there is no intent to harm another person, but one proceeds intentionally in a manner that infringes on the rights of another, a tort is committed. The law grants to each individual certain rights that must be respected by others. If by action or speech these rights are violated, resulting in injury, a tort has been committed.

The most common forms of intentional torts affecting school personnel include the following: assault, battery, defamation, false imprisonment, and trespass to personal property. (See the discussion of libel and slander in Chapter 6.)

Mental Distress

Causing mental distress is associated with liability. Charges of mental distress usually arise when one exhibits conduct that violates the acceptable boundaries of decency. It is a form of tort construed to create mental distress in the absence of some type of physical injury. Historically, it has been difficult to prove mental distress in the absence of some type of physical injury. However, this situation has changed in recent years.

School personnel may be charged with mental distress if there is evidence that their behavior or conduct was calculated to cause serious emotional distress for students. School personnel typically are charged with inflicting mental distress when they use an unreasonable and unorthodox method of discipline designed to embarrass students or cause them to be ridiculed or humiliated in the presence of their peers.

As previously stated in Chapter 5, courts will allow school personnel to discipline students as long as the discipline is reasonable and consistent with school or district policy. Many legal experts believe that actions by school personnel designed to embarrass students may be more damaging than physical harm. A student's self-esteem may be seriously damaged at a time when it should be growing and expanding. This is not intended to suggest that teachers or administrators cannot admonish a student in the classroom or hallway in front of his or her peers but, rather, to caution them to exercise prudent judgment in doing so.

A teacher, however, may be held liable if the evidence reveals that an intentional act was committed with the intent to humiliate or degrade when that act is accompanied by proof of wantonness or malice.[5] For example, an Ohio teacher faced mental distress and liability charges when she grabbed, choked, and shoved a first-grader in the school's lunch line in front of the rest of his class. The teacher exercised poor judgment and willful, wanton, and reckless conduct in dealing with the student.[6]

False Imprisonment

False imprisonment occurs when a student is detained illegally by the teacher or the principal. False imprisonment is considered to be an intentional tort. Wrongfully detaining a student for an unreasonable amount of time for offensive behavior that does not warrant detention constitutes a tort. School personnel must have a reasonable basis for confining a student, and the confinement must be viewed as reasonable. School or district policy should serve as a guide in these situations.

Teachers and administrators may detain students and prevent their participation in playground activities, recess, and certain other extracurricular activities. They may detain students after school if the offense is clearly one that warrants detention based on policy. Parents should be aware of the planned detention so that proper arrangements can be made to transport the student after the detention period has ended. Students should never be denied lunch breaks as a form of punishment. False imprisonment is not considered a major liability issue but is one that could prove difficult for school personnel if evidence reveals that detention was in violation of school or district policy and was carried out recklessly with malice toward the student.

Trespassing on Personal Property

Trespassing on personal property is a tort that involves confiscating or interfering with the use of a student's personal property, without proper authority. This is not an area that normally generates legal action but one that school personnel should be mindful of because it most commonly involves teachers and administrators.

This intentional tort occurs frequently when school personnel confiscate various items from students during the school day. Many of these items may be in violation of school rules, may create disruption, or may cause harm to the student in possession of the item or to other students.

Teachers and administrators have the right to confiscate such items, but they do not have the right to retain them for an unreasonable length of time. If an item is considered dangerous, the student's parent or guardian should be contacted and informed of the potential danger. Arrangements should be made with the parent or guardian to ensure that the item is not returned to the student to bring to school again.

UNINTENTIONAL TORTS

An unintentional tort is a wrong perpetrated by someone who fails to exercise that degree of care in doing what is otherwise permissible (that is, someone who acts negligently). Negligence is perhaps the most prevalent source of litigation involving injury to students. Many cases of negligence in school settings are often class actions, implicating teachers, administrators, and boards of education. Defendants in these cases are usually released from the suit if facts reveal that they played no significant role in the injury.

Negligence is generally viewed as the failure to exercise a reasonable standard of care, thereby resulting in harm or injury to another person. Most negligence cases involve civil wrongs, although there may be instances in which the accused faces both civil and criminal charges. In cases involving wanton negligence, such as injuries sustained by others as a result of violation of traffic laws, criminal charges may be appropriate, depending on the specific circumstances relating to the injury.

For example, when charges of negligence are sought by an injured student, certain requirements must be met. The student bringing the charges must be able to prove that four elements were present. Failure to establish each of the following four elements invalidates charges of liability.

Standard of Care

The teacher or administrator owes a legal duty to protect the student by conforming to certain standards. *Standard of care* is an important concept in cases involving liability of school personnel. It requires that school personnel exercise the same degree of care that a person of ordinary prudence would exercise under the same or similar conditions. This standard of care varies, depending on particular circumstances. The level of care due to students changes according to the age, maturity, experience, and mental capacity of students, as well as the nature of the learning activities in which they are involved.

Breach of Duty

Breach of duty occurs when the teacher or administrator fails to meet these standards—their duty of care. Breach of duty is determined in part by the nature of the activity for which the educator is held responsible. Various school activities require different levels of supervision. The first question normally posed by courts regarding breach is whether the conduct of school personnel met the standard of care required in a given situation. The second question is whether school personnel should have foreseen possible injury and taken appropriate steps to prevent it.

Proximity, or Legal Cause

The student must be able to demonstrate *proximate cause* (i.e., that a causal relationship existed between the breach of duty and the actual injury sustained by the student). If a student is injured and the injury is not related to the teacher's or administrator's failure to exercise the proper standard of care, there is no liability. There must be evidence that links the injury directly to the failure of educators to act prudently in a given situation.

Injury

The student must prove actual *injury* resulting from a breach of duty by the teacher or administrator. There must be evidence that actual injury resulted either from acts committed by school personnel or by their failure to act prudently in a given situation. If the student does not suffer harm or injury, there is no liability.

DEFENSES AGAINST NEGLIGENCE

Various defenses are used by school personnel to reduce or eliminate the impact of liability charges. These defenses are used even in cases where the four elements of negligence (listed previously) are present.

Contributory Negligence

Contributory negligence occurs when the injured party contributes to the injury because of poor decisions or actions. Contributory negligence is probably the most common defense employed against charges of negligence. When a teacher or administrator is charged with negligence, neither will be assessed monetary penalties when contributory negligence is proven. However, there is a common-law presumption that students cannot be charged with contributory negligence. This common-law precedent applies unconditionally to a child under the age of 7. Children between the ages of 7 and 14 are reasonably assumed to be incapable of contributory negligence. A child beyond the age of 14 is subject to charges of contributory negligence, depending on the facts surrounding the injury.

These age limits are not absolute. They typically serve as guides in assessing whether contributory negligence did occur.

Assumption of Risk

Assumption of risk is commonly used as a defense in situations involving various types of contact activities such as those engaged in by athletic teams, pep squads, and certain intramural activities. The theory supporting an assumption of risk is that students assume an element of risk when they choose to participate in and benefit from an activity. Even though a student assumes an element of risk, this does not relieve school personnel when they fail to meet a reasonable standard of care based on the age and maturity of the student, the risk, and the nature of the activity with which the risk is associated.

Comparative Negligence

Comparative negligence, a relatively new concept, has grown in popularity in many states. It differs from contributory negligence in that slight negligence by the plaintiff or injured party does not relieve the defendant or persons who may have greatly contributed to the injury.

Under *comparative negligence*, acts of those responsible are compared in the *degree of negligence* attributed in an injury situation. Juries normally determine the degree of negligence, which may range from slight to ordinary to gross, depending on the circumstances. The jury makes a determination regarding the degree to which each party contributed to an injury. If one party is found to have contributed more heavily to an injury than another, then that party is assessed a greater proportion for damages. Comparative negligence does not prevent recovery by the injured party but merely reduces the damages awarded, according to the degree of fault of the injured persons.

Immunity

The use of immunity as a legal defense has diminished and has not received strong support from the courts. *Immunity* is based on the view that the state and federal governments are protected from suits and cannot be held liable for injuries that result from the proper execution of governmental functions. Even in a few states where immunity is recognized, teachers are held liable for their individual acts that result in harm to students.

Liability Costs

School personnel are well advised to affiliate with their state and national educational associations, because membership carries liability protection for its members during the execution of their professional duties. Obviously, this benefit should not be the primary motivation for becoming affiliated but should be considered as an important aspect of membership.

DUTIES OF SUPERVISION

All teachers and administrators are expected to reasonably supervise students under their charge. The degree of supervision will vary with each situation. The less mature students are, the greater the need for supervision. The greater the potential for injury to students engaging in certain activities, the greater the need for supervision.

Whether school personnel have adequately fulfilled their duty of supervision is a question of fact for a jury to decide.

Each case rests on its merits. Courts will consider such factors as the nature of the activity involved, the age and number of students engaged in the activity, and the quality of supervision.

Supervision Before and After School

School personnel have a responsibility to provide some form of supervision for students who arrive on campus before the normal school day begins. The amount of supervision depends on the circumstances involving early arrival of students. Foreseeability is established when a group of students arrives early or remains on campus after school without some form of supervision. Teachers and administrators are expected to foresee that students might be harmed if no form of supervision is provided. The same principle applies to students who are detained on campus after school, waiting for their parents to arrive. Once foreseeability has been established, it is necessary to take reasonable and prudent measures.

There is no expectation that teachers and administrators guarantee that students will never be injured on school grounds. Certainly, this would be impossible to achieve. What must be demonstrated, however, is that reasonable measures were taken to prevent foreseeable harm to students. For example, there would be no expectation that teachers and administrators would arrive or remain on campus during unreasonable hours to provide supervision. Although the courts have not addressed the time frame issue per se, it might be a factor in deciding whether teachers or administrators failed to meet a reasonable standard of supervision.

Certainly, parents should be informed in writing that school personnel are not available during the very early morning hours or later afternoon to supervise students. Parents should be discouraged from bringing their children to campus during early hours and encouraged to pick them up promptly after school. Although these steps should be taken, they do not in themselves totally relieve teachers and administrators of supervisory responsibilities. The courts will usually reason that students are not present on campus during the hours before and after school by their own choice. They are there because of parental decisions.

Administrators have the responsibility for ensuring that the campus is safe for early-arriving students. Students and their parents should be informed of the behavior expected of students when they arrive before or remain after school. Once students are informed, some form of periodic supervision should be provided to ensure that students are exhibiting proper conduct and are not engaged in potentially harmful activities.

Field Trips

School-sponsored field trips are considered to be mere extensions of normal school activities and thus require a reasonable standard of supervision by school personnel. In many instances, special supervision is required, because students visit unfamiliar places that trigger a greater need for supervision. Field trip activities generally provide valuable learning experiences for students. Because schools are moving toward connecting classroom learning to real-life situations, school-sponsored field trips will likely increase in popularity and instructional value.

Teachers are expected to exercise reasonable standards of supervision during field trip experiences. Students should be informed prior to actual field trip excursions of the circumstances surrounding each trip. If there are special instructions or concerns, they should be properly conveyed by the teacher who has responsibility for supervising the field trip. Students, as well as parents, particularly those whose children are enrolled in the lower grades, should be informed of rules and expected behavior during the activity.

The standard of care involving field trips will vary, depending on the age and maturity of students and the nature of the field trip experience. Teachers who organize field trips and administrators who approve them should be certain that there is adequate supervision in terms of *quality* and *quantity*. For example, it is foreseeable that if one teacher attempts to supervise 50 young, immature students during a trip to the zoo, a student might be harmed if an insufficient number of chaperones are not available to assist with supervisory duties.

It is an acceptable practice to request that parents serve as chaperones during these excursions, in which case parents should be fully informed of the nature of the activities involved, the type of students who will be supervised, and specific instructions regarding their supervisory duties. Students who are extremely active or have a history of misbehavior should be closely supervised by the classroom teacher, as it is foreseeable that they may be injured under certain conditions.

If field trips are well organized and supervised, they will meet the standard of care expected of school personnel while providing a valuable learning experience for students.

Parental Consent and Written Waivers

It is a common practice for school districts to require parents to sign permission slips allowing their children to participate in certain school-sponsored activities away from the school. This practice may have obvious value, as parents are involved in the decision-making process regarding these activities.

In some cases, these consent forms also contain a waiver or a disclosure statement that relieves the school of any legal responsibility in the event a student is injured during a field-based school-sponsored activity. This practice might psychologically discourage a parent who has endorsed such a form from raising a legal challenge in the event of an injury to his or her child, but it does not in any way relieve school personnel of their duty to provide reasonable supervision. Such forms have very limited, if any, legal authority. If a parent grants permission for the child to engage in an activity and also signs a waiver, legal action based on a lack of proper supervision may still be brought against school personnel for negligence that resulted in an injury to a student. Teachers should be aware that permission forms, although valuable, do not abrogate their legal duty to supervise and provide for the safety of students during these excursions. Depending on the statute of limitations, it also is probable that a student may later bring suit against the district when he or she reaches majority age, even if the parent elects not to do so at the time the student was injured.

Parent Chaperones and Liability

Parent chaperones may provide a valuable service to public schools during field trip excursions. However, parents must ensure that all school rules and policies governing field trips are understood and followed judiciously. Additionally, chaperones must be informed by school personnel regarding the nature of the field trip experience, the number of students they are expected to supervise, and any challenges associated with the trip. Standards of care must be clearly spelled out regarding chaperones' responsibility for student safety. Parents must foresee potential danger and ensure that students are protected from harm. Chaperones may be held liable for acts of negligence and failure to meet the prescribed standard of care necessary to protect students. The age and maturity of participating students will affect the required standard of care. Depending on school district policy, chaperones may or may not be allowed to travel on school-sponsored transportation. Typically, some parents voluntarily drive their personal vehicles in the event of an emergency. Some school districts provide liability coverage, whereas others do not.

GUIDES

School Liability

1. School district personnel must be aware of the standard of care that must be met in all activities as they instruct and supervise students in various activities to which they have been assigned.
2. Every teacher or administrator has a responsibility to ensure to the fullest extent possible that school buildings and grounds are safe for student use.
3. The absence of foreseeability as a defense by school personnel will not be upheld by the courts when the facts reveal that school personnel were expected to foresee the potential danger of a situation that resulted in injury to a student.
4. Teachers have a legal duty to properly instruct, supervise, and provide a safe environment for students.
5. Reasonable and prudent decisions regarding student safety usually will withstand court scrutiny.
6. A higher standard of care may be expected of teachers during field trips and excursions involving students, especially in cases when students are viewed as licensees (that is, when they are on property for their own purpose, with actual or implied consent).
7. Students should not be coerced into using equipment or performing a physical activity for which they express serious apprehension. Coercion of this type could result in injury to the student and liability charges against school personnel.
8. Teachers and administrators should be reminded that the infliction of mental distress on students may result in personal liability charges.
9. The conduct of school personnel should not be calculated to cause emotional harm to students.
10. When possible, interactions with students and teachers that might tend to embarrass the students or create mental distress should occur in private and not in the presence of the students' peers.
11. Board of education members may be held liable for their individual acts that result in the violation of a student's rights.

12. Students should not be detained after school for unreasonable amounts of time for behavior that does not warrant detention.

13. Items retrieved from students, if not illegal, should be returned to students or their parents within a reasonable time frame and not retained permanently by school personnel.

14. A higher standard of care is necessary in laboratories, in physical education classes, during contact sports, and on field trips.

15. Parent chaperones should be informed of potential liability challenges when they commit intentional or unintentional acts involving students during field trip excursions.

16. School officials should provide some form of supervision for students arriving before the school day begins or departing after the school day ends.

PRACTICAL TIPS

Do:

1. Take reasonable measures to protect students from unreasonable risk of harm. Failure to do so may result in student injury and liability challenges.

2. Exercise your responsibility to anticipate foreseeable dangers for your students, and take necessary measures to protect students in your care. Teachers have a duty to foresee potential danger involving students.

3. Provide students with adequate instruction prior to allowing them to participate in any activity that may be potentially dangerous, such as laboratory experiments, the use of shop equipment, during contact sports, or other, similar activities. Follow through with appropriate supervision of these activities to minimize the potential for harm to students.

4. Maintain a safe classroom by conducting daily inspections and identifying faulty desks or equipment that may endanger students. Report potentially unsafe conditions appropriately.

Do not:

1. Leave students unsupervised unless it is absolutely necessary. If students must be left alone, use other measures, such as ensuring that they are monitored by a fellow teacher in an adjacent classroom.

2. Send students on errands off school grounds, irrespective of their ages. Teachers are responsible for students if they are injured, even though a student may have used poor judgment in sustaining an injury.

3. Allow students to wander away from a supervised group while engaged in a field trip experience. It is foreseeable that they may be exposed to risk of injury when unsupervised in an unfamiliar environment.

4. Use your personal vehicle to transport students unless it is absolutely necessary. Liability charges may be imminent if wanton negligence is proven in an accident that results in injury to a student.

5. Fail to assist an injured student even when he or she is not directly under your supervision. The degree of assistance should be based on your training and experience, as well as the nature of the injury and the immediate need to act on the student's behalf.

ENDNOTES

1. *Mitchell v. Forsyth*, 472 U.S. 511, 105 S. Ct. 2806 (1985).
2. *Davis v. Scherer*, 468 U.S, 183 104 S. Ct. 3012 (1984).
3. Restatement of Torts, Second § 339.
4. *Jackson v. Cartwright School District*, 607 P.2d 975 (Ariz. 1980).
5. *Gordon v. Oak Park School District No. 97*, 24 Ill. App. 3d 131, 320 N.E.2d 389 (1974).
6. *Rogers v. Akron City School System No. CV 2006-05-2869*, 2008 WL 2439674 (Ohio Ct. App. 6/18/08).

9

Discrimination in Employment

Constitutional, federal, and state statutes prohibit discriminatory practices in employment on the basis of sex, race, age, color, or religion. A significant number of federal statutes have specifically been enacted to address discrimination in employment. The social and political movements during the early 1960s focused major attention on inequalities of employment opportunities and past discrimination practices. Many important pieces of federal legislation were enacted during the 1960s and 1970s, one of the most significant of which was Title VII of the Civil Rights Act of 1964, which prohibits employment discrimination based on race, color, religion, sex, or national origin.

The equal protection clause of the Fourteenth Amendment, which provides protection against group discrimination and unfair treatment, is used as a vehicle for individuals who seek relief from various forms of discrimination. A significant number of personnel practices in public schools pertaining to race, gender, age, and religion have been challenged by allegations of discrimination. Many school districts have responded to these challenges by noting that many of their current practices have been based on custom rather than a deliberate intent to discriminate. Nonetheless, courts have responded to challenges brought by school personnel in cases regarding alleged discrimination in employment practices based on issues involving gender, race, age, and pregnancy.

TITLE VII: DISCRIMINATION

One of the most extensive federal employment laws, the Civil Rights Act of 1964, Title VII, provides, in part, that

    A. It shall be an unlawful employment practice for any employee

1. *to fail or refuse to hire or to discharge any individual or otherwise to discriminate against any individual with respect to his compensation, terms and conditions or privileges of employment, because of such individual's race, color, religion, sex or national origin;*

2. *to limit, segregate or classify his employees or applicants for employment in any way which would deprive or tend to deprive any individual of employment opportunities or otherwise adversely affect his status as an employee, because of such individual's race, color, religion, sex or national origin.*

B. *It shall be an unlawful employment practice for an employment agency to fail or refuse to refer for employment, or otherwise to discriminate against any individual, because of his race, color, religion, sex or national origin, or to classify or refer for employment any individual on the basis of his race, color, religion, sex or national origin.*[1]

The original statute covered employers and labor unions and did not apply to discriminatory employment practices in educational institutions until 1972, when the law was amended. Since its amendment, it has been utilized by educators to challenge questionable discriminatory practices in public schools. As stipulated in Titles VII and IX, discrimination in employment based on gender is prohibited. Title VII protects males and females from gender-based discrimination.

Title VII was amended by the Civil Rights Act of 1991 (P.L. 102-166). This act provides for compensatory damages, punitive damages, and jury trial in cases involving intentional discrimination. An individual claiming discrimination under Title VII must file a complaint with the Equal Employment Opportunity Commission (EEOC) within 180 days following the alleged unlawful employment practice or within 300 days if the individual has filed a claim with a local or state civil rights agency. Failure to meet these time limits will result in a loss of legal standing to challenge the alleged act. Remedies available under Title VII include compensatory damages, punitive damages, back pay, and reinstatement (for disparate treatment and incrimination), which are discussed later in this chapter.

To succeed under Title VII, a plaintiff must demonstrate that the employer's reason for the challenged employment decision is false and that the actual reason is discrimination. This burden is often difficult to prove, because there are very few instances in which plaintiffs have objective evidence or proof of discrimination. Many, however, have succeeded with indirect proof of discrimination, in which the pretext for discrimination is established and the defendant is unable to convince the court that the reasons for his or her actions are worthy of belief.

Under the law of discrimination, for example, a plaintiff teacher or administrator must demonstrate that he or she has made application for a position, is qualified for the position, and was not given fair consideration for the position. If the teacher or administrator is able to demonstrate a bona fide case of discrimination, then the burden shifts to the school district to demonstrate that its employment decision was not based on discriminatory practices.

In two historic noneducation cases, *McDonnell Douglas Corp. v. Green*[2] in 1973 and *Furnco Construction Corp. v. Waters*[3] in 1978, the Supreme Court developed a three-step procedure for Title VII challenges:

1. The plaintiff carries the initial burden of establishing a prima facie case of employment discrimination.
2. The burden shifts to the defendant to refute the prima facie case by demonstrating that a legitimate, nondiscriminatory purpose forms the basis for its actions.
3. If the defendant is successful in its contention, then the burden shifts back to the plaintiff to show that the defendant's actions were a mere pretext for discrimination. If, of course, the defendant can demonstrate the absence of a discriminatory motive, there is no need for step three.[4]

In a race discrimination case, the U.S. Court of Appeals for the Fifth Circuit held that a Mississippi school board did not discriminate against a 57-year-old African American female applicant by hiring a "young white female" for a principal's position. The applicant did not perform well in her interview and did not prove that the board's use of the interview was discriminatory. The board used standardized questions for the interviews and selected the candidate who received the highest score.[5]

In a sexual orientation case, the U.S. Court of Appeals for the Seventh Circuit stated that homosexuals do not enjoy a heightened level of constitutional protection. Title VII does not provide a private right of action based on sexual orientation discrimination, and there is no remedy under

42 U.S.C. § 1983 for discrimination based on sexual orientation, according to rights created under Title VII.[6]

Although these are not education cases, the same procedures apply in all cases involving alleged discrimination, including those in public schools.

Sexual Discrimination

Discrimination based on sex is covered under Title IX of the Education Amendments Act of 1972, 20 U.S.C. § 1681 et seq., which prohibits sexual discrimination by public and private education institutions receiving federal funds. The basic provision of the act states, "No person in the United States shall on the basis of sex, be excluded from participation in, be denied the benefits of, or be subjected to discrimination under any educational program or activity receiving federal financial assistance."[7]

Title IX is administered by the Office for Civil Rights (OCR) of the Department of Education. The provisions of this act are similar to those in EEOC's guidelines found in Title VII. Title IX, like Title VII, makes a provision for sexual distinctions in employment where sex is a bona fide occupational qualification.[8] During the mid-1970s, educational institutions raised numerous challenges questioning the applicability of Title IX to discrimination in employment issues. After a series of highly debated cases, the U.S. Supreme Court ruled in *North Haven Board of Education v. Bell* in 1988 that Title IX does apply to and does prohibit sexual discrimination in employment.[9] It is important to note that the terms *sex* and *gender* may be used interchangeably. However, sex typically refers to biological differences based on chromosomes, whereas gender generally describes characteristics that society or a certain culture demarcates as masculine or feminine.

THE REHABILITATION ACT OF 1973 AND THE AMERICANS WITH DISABILITIES ACT OF 1990

The Americans with Disabilities Act (ADA) protects individuals with disabilities against discrimination and ensures equal access and opportunity (see Chapter 7, "Individuals with Disabilities"). Section 504 of the Rehabilitation Act of 1973 prohibits discrimination with respect to employment, training, compensation, promotion, fringe benefits, and terms and conditions of employment against any otherwise qualified person who has a disability. The act states that "no otherwise qualified individual with handicaps . . . shall solely by reason of his or her handicap be excluded from the participation in, be denied the benefits of, or be subjected to discrimination under any program or activity receiving federal financial assistance. . . ."[10] The ADA is similar to Section 504 and protects not only students with disabilities but any person who has a physical or mental impairment that substantially limits one or more major life activities, has a record of such impairment, or is regarded by others as having such an impairment.[11]

Major life activities, as interpreted by the act, may include caring for oneself, performing manual tasks, hearing, seeing, speaking, breathing, walking, learning, and working.[12] Section 504 extends beyond the school environment and covers all persons with disabilities in any program receiving federal financial assistance. Contrary to popular belief, the Rehabilitation Act does not require affirmative action on behalf of people with disabilities; all that it requires is the guarantee of equal opportunity.

The ADA Amendments Act of 2008 made important changes to the definition of the term *disability*. See Table 9.1 for significant changes to the act.

The ADA Amendments Act became effective on January 1, 2009.

Qualifications for Employment

Any individual with a disability is *qualified*, under ADA, if, with or without reasonable accommodations, he or she can perform the core functions of the employment position held or desired to be held. Core job functions are not those considered marginal but, rather, those essential to successfully executing the designated tasks. The act prohibits denying a job to any individual with a disability on the basis of the applicant's inability to meet physical or mental tasks that are not essential to effectively performing the job tasks. School boards, therefore, must make reasonable accommodations to any known physical or mental impairment of an otherwise qualified individual with a disability. An employer may be exempt if it can be demonstrated that an undue hardship is involved in making a reasonable accommodation.

The term *undue hardship* means an action requiring significant difficulty or expense when considered in light of the following factors:

1. *the nature and cost of the accommodation needed under this act;*

TABLE 9.1 Summary of Major Changes Under the Reauthorized Americans With Disabilities Act Amendments Act of 2008

Key Revisions	
1. Provides broader scope of protection.	Mitigating measures such as medications and other interventions that manage a disease must be ignored.
2. Overturns U.S. Supreme Court cases that held that mitigating measures must be considered in determining an impairment.	Decisions in *Sutton v. United Airlines, Albertson's v. Kirkingburg,* and *Murphy v. United Parcel* eliminating correctable illnesses under ADA coverage are not valid in determining an impairment.
3. Expands definition of major life activities.	Major life activities such as operation of major bodily functions related to the immune, respiratory, neurological systems and food allergies have been added.
4. Lowers the bar for ADA coverage.	EEOC regulations that construe *substantially limits* to mean *significantly or severely restricted* have been rejected.
5. Expands coverage to include episodic impairments.	A person who experiences episodic impairments is protected even when the person is in remission. Examples include multiple sclerosis, lupus, epilepsy, or seizure disorders.

Source: The Reauthorized Americans with Disabilities Act Amendments Act of 2008.

2. *the overall financial resources of the facility or facilities involved in the provision of the reasonable accommodation, the number of persons employed at such facility, the effect on expenses and resources, or any other impacts of such accommodation upon the operation of the facility;*

3. *the overall financial resources of the covered entity, the overall size of the business of a covered entity with respect to the number of its employees, and the number, type, and location of its facilities; and*

4. *the type of operation or operations of the covered entity, including the composition, structure, and*

> *functions of the work force of the entity, as well as the*
> *geographic separateness and administrative or fiscal*
> *relationship of the facility or facilities in question to*
> *the covered entity.*[13]

The burden of proof clearly rests with the employer.

Scope of Protection—Section 504 and the ADA

Both the ADA and the rehabilitation acts affect public schools by prohibiting *disability-based discrimination*. When an allegation claiming discrimination is brought against a school district, individuals bringing such a charge may file a complaint with the Department of Education. If a violation is found, the Department of Education can mandate that federal funds be terminated, subject to judicial review of such action. Affected individuals also may seek relief in the courts for such violations. Available remedies may include injunctive relief and, possibly, monetary damages when there is evidence of malicious intent or bad faith in discriminating against individuals with disabilities.

GUIDES

Americans with Disabilities

1. The ADA prohibits employment discrimination by employers with 15 or more employees.
2. School districts should develop nondiscriminatory policies regarding individuals with disabilities.
3. School districts should not segregate or limit job opportunities for individuals on the basis of their disability.
4. School districts shall not utilize and promote standards that have a discriminatory effect on, or that perpetuate discrimination against, persons with disabilities.
5. School officials shall not deny employment to individuals with disabilities to avoid providing reasonable accommodations.
6. School districts must utilize standards that identify the skills of a person with a disability rather than his or her impairments.
7. School districts should take appropriate measures to protect the confidentiality of medical records regarding individuals with disabilities.
8. School districts may be assessed compensatory and punitive damages for deliberate acts of discrimination against individuals with disabilities.

Racial Discrimination

After the landmark 1954 *Brown v. Board of Education*[14] case, court-ordered desegregation resulted in numerous challenges of racial discrimination, as predominantly black schools were closed and teachers and administrators were reassigned to other schools. In many instances, blacks who held significant administrative positions prior to court-ordered desegregation found themselves in lower positions or nonadministrative positions during the aftermath of the desegregation movement. Even though the courts, by their rulings, attempted to achieve some degree of equity in assignment of blacks to predominantly white schools, their efforts fell short of achieving this objective.

Blacks relied on the equal protection clause of the Fourteenth Amendment to eradicate patterns of racial discrimination in public schools. The equal protection standards prohibited discrimination that could be linked with a racially motivated objective.[15] Unlike with Title VII, no remedial action was attached to the equal protection clause unless there was clear evidence that segregation was de jure (that is, unless official and deliberate laws or policies promoted segregation).

Title VII involves two basic types of claims: disparate treatment and disparate impact. *Disparate treatment* simply means that an employer treats some people more unfavorably than others regarding employment, job promotion, or employment conditions on the basis of race, color, religion, sex, or national origin. *Disparate impact* is merely a demonstration that numbers of people of a similar class are affected adversely by a particular employment practice that appears neutral, such as a requirement that all employees pass a test. The protected class categories usually include race, gender, religion, and national origin. Disparate impact lawsuits differ from disparate treatment suits in that they do not allege overt discriminatory action.

Religious Discrimination

The First Amendment and Title VII provide protection to employees against religious discrimination. Religion is defined by Title VII to include all aspects of religious observances, practices, and beliefs. Under this act, employers are expected to make reasonable accommodations to an employee's religious observance unless a hardship can be demonstrated. The burden of proof rests with the employer to demonstrate undue hardship. Most states have enacted legislation that requires employers to make accommodations for employees' religious practices. Thus, employers must exercise caution to ensure that the religious rights of employees are not violated. Employers also must be certain that the establishment clause of the First Amendment is not violated as well.

Age Discrimination

Age discrimination in public schools primarily affects teachers. In past years, many districts forced teachers to retire on reaching a specified age. These policies and practices were challenged by teachers under equal protection guarantees. Many of these challenges received mixed reviews by the courts. For example, the U.S. Supreme Court supported mandatory retirement for police officers because of the rigorous physical demands associated with their positions. By contrast, the U.S. Court of Appeals for the Seventh Circuit rejected a practice of forced retirement for teachers at age 65, noting that there was no justification to presume that teachers at age 65 lacked the academic skill or intellectual or physical rigor to teach.[16]

All challenges and uncertainties became insignificant with the passage of the Age Discrimination in Employment Act of 1967 (ADEA) as amended in 1978. This act effectively prohibits the forced retirement of employees by protecting people above age 40 from discrimination on the basis of age with respect to hiring, dismissal, and other terms and conditions of employment. Prior to the act's amendment in 1978, the maximum age limit was set at 65. The 1978 amendment raised the limit to 70. Amendments added in 1986 removed the limit completely except for persons in certain public safety positions (e.g., police officers and firefighters). The act covers teachers and other public employees. Many districts have implemented early-retirement incentive plans, and these are generally held acceptable by the courts if they are strictly voluntary in nature. There can be no evidence that any force or coercion was used to enforce such plans. Currently, mandatory retirement plans for employees of public schools, colleges, and universities are prohibited. Universities were exempt until 1993, but they must now comply with the law.

HIV Positive Teachers in Public Schools

Teachers who carry the AIDS virus, HIV, have a right to teach as long as they do not pose a health risk to students or colleagues, or their ability to be effective teachers is not impaired.

Consequently, they cannot be discriminated against on the basis of their illness. There should be no inquiries regarding whether a teacher is HIV-positive. In fact, an HIV positive teacher is protected by privacy laws; consequently, employees are not permitted to divulge whether an employee is HIV-positive. HIV research has shown that there is little risk that an HIV-positive teacher will infect students or colleagues. AIDS is viewed as a long-term illness that is managed with proper medication.

Schools and Transgender Teachers

Experts estimate that there are fewer than 30 transgender teachers in classrooms nationwide. Nevertheless, they should be treated like any other employee. Teachers may exercise freedom of choice even in the context of a sexual transformation. School leaders with transgender teachers in their schools should hold information sessions with students and parents to respond to any issues and concerns regarding transgender issues. It is not necessary that the school embrace transgender values, but it is important to ensure that transgender teachers are treated with fairness and respect. It is important to note that it is illegal to discriminate against an individual on the basis of gender.

PREGNANCY AND PUBLIC SCHOOL EMPLOYMENT

Teachers in public schools are protected by the Pregnancy Discrimination Act of 1978 (P.L. 95-555). This law amends Title VII to extend protection to pregnant employees against any forms of discrimination based on pregnancy. The courts have been fairly consistent in their rulings regarding issues related to pregnancy. Prior to the enactment of P.L. 95-555, it was not uncommon for districts to enforce policy cutoff dates by which females were required to leave their positions owing to their pregnant status. In a significant 1974 case, *Cleveland Board of Education v. LaFleur*,[17] the court held that mandatory maternity-related termination specifying the number of months before anticipated childbirth violated the equal protection clause of the Fourteenth Amendment and noted that arbitrary cutoff dates served no legitimate state interest in maintaining a continuous and orderly instructional program.

Districts may not assume that every teacher is physically unable to perform her teaching duties and responsibilities effectively because she is pregnant at a specific point in time.

Courts have also not been supportive of district policies that barred a female teacher, after giving birth, from returning to the district until the next regular semester or year. Female teachers have also brought numerous challenges regarding disability benefits, sick leave, and adequate insurance coverage.

Many of these challenges led to the enactment of the Pregnancy Discrimination Act. The basic intent of the act is to ensure that pregnant employees are treated in the same manner as other employees with respect to the ability to perform their duties. The act covers pregnancy, childbirth, and related medical conditions. Under this act, a woman can no longer be legally dismissed or denied a job or promotion owing to pregnancy. Women must be able to use sick leave, as do other employees for other health conditions, and return to work when they are released by their physicians. Pregnancy must be treated as a temporary condition, thus entitling female employees to the same provisions of disability benefits, sick leave, and insurance coverage as any other employee who has a temporary disability.

FAMILY AND MEDICAL LEAVE ACT

The Family and Medical Leave Act (FMLA) was passed by Congress in 1993 and revised in 2009. It is designed to allow eligible employees up to a total of 12 workweeks of unpaid leave during any 12-month period for one or more of the following reasons:

1. the birth and care of the newborn child of the employee;
2. placement with the employee of a son or daughter for adoption or foster care;
3. to care for an immediate family member (spouse, child, or parent) with a serious health condition; and
4. to take medical leave when the employee is unable to work because of a serious health condition.

Employers with 50 or more employees are covered by this act. An eligible employee is a worker who has been employed for at least 12 months or for at least 1,250 hours over the previous 12 months. The law permits an employee to elect, or the employer to require the employee, to use accrued paid leave, such as vacation or sick leave, for some or all of the FMLA leave period. When paid leave is substituted for unpaid FMLA leave, it may be counted against the 12-week FMLA leave entitlement if the employer is properly notified of the designation when the leave begins.

An employer may ask the employee to confirm whether the leave requested or being taken is qualified for FMLA purposes. An employer's requirement of periodic reports regarding the employee's status and intent to return to work after a leave of absence is permissible under the act. If an employer wishes to obtain another medical opinion, the affected employee may be required to secure additional medical certification at the employer's expense.

GUIDES

Discrimination

1. Punitive damages may be awarded in employment discrimination cases if the employer's conduct is viewed as egregious.
2. School districts will not be supported by the courts when there is evidence that their actions discriminated against employees on the basis of race, color, religion, gender, or national origin.
3. Once prima facie evidence is presented by the employee affected, school officials must demonstrate that a compelling education interest motivated their decisions.
4. School districts may not discriminate against employees because employees opposed practices made unlawful under discrimination laws or participated in an investigation regarding employment discrimination.
5. School officials may be held liable in any cases involving discrimination or harassment when it is determined that they were aware or should have been aware of these actions.
6. No employee may be coerced to retire from an employment position on the basis of age, nor may the employee, because of the employee's age, be denied rights and privileges afforded other employees, such as promotion and other benefits.
7. Race discrimination affects all employees, not merely minority employees.
8. Differential employment criteria that have an adverse effect on a special group of employees shall not be used, even though these criteria may appear to be neutral.
9. Teachers and school personnel are entitled to rights under FMLA if they meet eligibility criteria.
10. It is unlawful for any employer to interfere with, restrain, or deny the exercise of any right provided to employees under FMLA.

11. HIV-positive teachers have a right to teach as long as they do not pose a health risk to others.
12. Transgender teachers are protected against discrimination based on gender.

SEXUAL HARASSMENT

Sexual harassment is prohibited by Titles VII and IX. In spite of these prohibitions, incidents of sexual harassment continue to grow at alarming rates. Cases involving charges of sexual harassment have increased rather dramatically in recent years. According to statistics filed with the EEOC, sexual harassment charges more than doubled over a 4-year period.

Interestingly, sexual harassment was not included in Title VII of the Civil Rights Amendment of 1964 until 1980. Its primary intent is to protect employees from harassment in their work environments. *Sexual harassment* is considered to be a form of sex discrimination. It can manifest itself in many forms, from verbal statements and physical gestures to overt behavior.

The victim, as well as the harasser, may be a male or a female. The victim need not be of the opposite sex. The victim may not be the person harassed but may be anyone affected by the offensive conduct. A claim of economic injury is not necessary to bring a successful case of harassment against a supervisor.

Various levels of verbal harassment behavior are recognized by the courts, including, but not limited to, making personal inquiries of a sexual nature, offering sexual comments regarding a person's anatomy or clothing, repeatedly requesting dates, and refusing to accept no as an answer. Nonverbal harassment may include prolonged staring at another person, presenting personal gifts without cause, throwing kisses or licking one's lips, making various sexual gestures with one's hand, or posting sexually suggestive cartoons or pictures.

More serious levels of sexual harassment may involve sexual coercion or unwanted physical relations. This type of behavior, quid pro quo, is commonly associated with superior–subordinate relationships in which the subordinate victim, for fear of reprisal, will unwillingly participate in sexual activities demanded by the superior. This relationship is best described as a power relationship in which, because of his or her position, the supervisor has the capacity, for example, to refuse to hire or promote the subordinate, or to grant or deny certain privileges. In many instances, the promise of some job-related benefit is offered in exchange for sexual favors.

Another level of harassment involves unwanted touching of another's hair, clothing, or body. Undesirable acts involving hugging, kissing, stroking, patting, or massaging one's neck or shoulders are examples of physical harassment that contribute to a hostile work environment. Verbal harassment may include making off-the-cuff comments, such as referring to females as *babe*, *honey*, or *sweetheart* or turning work discussions into sexual discussions including sexual jokes or stories.

Each of these levels represents a serious form of sexual discrimination for which the victim may recover damages. The burden rests with the victim to establish that the various levels of harassment described are unwanted. Once this has been established, the harasser has an obligation to discontinue such behavior immediately. Failure to do so usually creates a hostile work environment and results in charges of sexual harassment by the victim. The alleged victim sometimes finds it difficult to pursue sexual harassment claims in court. In many instances, embarrassing and graphic details must be revealed, and these are often denied by the person(s) against whom charges are made. Many victims of various forms of discrimination have been awarded monetary damages. The dollar amounts have increased significantly in recent years.

The definition of *harassment*, under the act, is sufficiently broad to cover most forms of unacceptable behavior. Any type of sexual behavior or advance that is unwanted or unwelcome is considered covered under the act. As indicated earlier, the person affected by such behavior has an obligation to inform the party that his or her behavior is unwanted or unwelcome. If this does not occur, it is difficult to claim harassment, because the accused party is assumed to be unaware that his or her behavior is unwelcome. Although the regulation implementing enforcement against sexual harassment is very broad, it is fairly prescriptive with respect to coverage. It defines *sexual harassment* in the following manner:

> *Unwelcome sexual advances, requests for sexual favors and other verbal or physical contact of a sexual nature constitute sexual harassment when (1) submission to such conduct is made either explicitly or implicitly a term or condition of an individual's employment (2) submission to or rejection of such conduct by an*

individual is used as the basis for employment decisions affecting such individuals or (3) such conduct has the purpose or effect of unreasonably interfering with an individual's work performance or creating an intimidating, hostile or offensive working environment.[18]

Legally, employees shall not be denied promotions or other benefits to which they are entitled on the basis of their unwillingness to tolerate sexual misconduct by their superiors, nor shall they be subjected to hostile, unfriendly environments by superiors or peers when they (the employees who are victims) refuse to tolerate sexual misconduct. Under the act, every person is entitled to an environment free of unwelcome sexual conduct and one that allows the person to perform his or her duties without intimidation or fear of reprisal.

EEOC guidelines cover two types of sexual harassment, previously mentioned: *quid pro quo* and *non–quid pro quo*. In *quid pro quo harassment*, an employee exchanges sexual favors for job benefits, promotion, or continued employment. In *non–quid pro quo*, or a hostile environment, the employee is subjected to a sexually hostile and intimidating work environment that psychologically affects the employee's well-being and has an adverse effect on his or her job performance.

A landmark case involving sexual harassment in the private sector involved a female bank employee who filed action against the bank and her supervisor, alleging that she had been subjected to sexual harassment by her supervisor during her employment, in violation of Title VII.

The supervisor's contention was that the sexual relationship was consensual and had no bearing on her continued employment. The bank indicated that it had no knowledge or notice of the allegation and therefore could not be held liable.

The Supreme Court, in the landmark 1986 ruling *Meritor Savings Bank v. Vinson* held that unwelcome sexual advances that create an offensive or hostile work environment violate Title VII.[19] It further held that whereas employers are not automatically liable for sexual harassment committed by their supervisors, absence of notice does not automatically insulate the employers from liability in such cases.

The significance of the ruling set the stage for subsequent sexual harassment cases by providing the definition of specific acts that fall within the category of harassment. The High Court suggested that Title VII guidelines are not limited to economic or tangible injuries. Harassment that leads to noneconomic injury may also violate Title VII. The court considered the employer's claim—that the sexual activity was voluntary—to be without merit. The test, according to the court, was whether such advances were unwelcome.

Sexual harassment is prevalent in the United States and will likely continue to present legal challenges. This issue continues to evolve in the courts, which are defining the legal limits of acceptable and unacceptable sex-related behavior in the workplace.

Sexual Harassment of Students by School Personnel

Sexual harassment of students by teachers and administrators is unacceptable behavior that will generally result in dismissal as well as criminal charges. Additionally, it may create serious and devastating consequences for students who are victims of such behavior. In the school setting, nonconsensual and consensual sexual interactions between students and school personnel are impermissible, violate professional standards of conduct, and may be viewed as harassment as an abuse of the power that teachers and administrators exercise over students. In all cases, teachers and administrators are expected to refrain from any sexual overtures toward students.

GUIDES

Sexual Harassment

1. District policies and procedures to address sexual harassment should be formulated for employees.
2. School officials should respond judiciously to any charges brought by employees regarding sexual harassment.
3. School officials should establish a zero tolerance policy so that everyone understands the school's position on issues involving harassment.
4. Development programs should be provided periodically for faculty and staff to familiarize them with all aspects of harassment and specific behaviors considered to be in the harassment category.
5. Faculty should be encouraged to report all violations through a well-defined, well-developed, and well-publicized grievance procedure.
6. School officials should create an environment in which school personnel feel comfortable in honestly reporting complaints of harassment, free from any form of reprisal.

7. The confidentiality of those filing complaints should be protected to the greatest degree possible. Professional reputations can be damaged if charges prove to be false.

8. Sexual harassment of students by school personnel is illegal and may result in dismissal of those personnel.

PRACTICAL TIPS

Do:

1. Make certain that you clearly understand all federal and state statutes banning discrimination. Knowledge of federal law protects teachers from treating students in an arbitrary and capricious manner and from similarly being mistreated by employers.

2. Understand that a teacher carries the initial burden to establish a valid claim of employment discrimination in cases alleging unfair employment practices. Burden of proof is often difficult to establish. Strong documentation is absolutely essential.

3. Understand that pregnancy may not be used against female teachers in any manner that deprives them of an employment position.

4. Be aware that correctable disabilities involving medication do qualify under the disabilities act. A recent federal statute provides ADA coverage for certain correctable disabilities.

5. Understand that your school district must not show preference for one religion over another or create advantages for some individuals and disadvantages for others on the basis of religious preferences. Since you are an employee of your school district, your religious rights must be respected to the greatest degree possible.

Do not:

1. Ignore the fact that sexual harassment may be a form of discrimination. If it involves teacher–student relations, it may result in serious disciplinary consequences, including dismissal.

2. Fail to report suspected violations of school or district harassment practices. Failure to do so may not only create a hostile environment for others but also result in harsh disciplinary actions by school officials.

3. Fail to create a classroom environment in which students are informed that harassing conduct is highly

inappropriate and unacceptable. Students must be informed of behavior that constitutes harassment.

4. Be afraid to participate in a discriminatory investigation, for fear of reprisal. Discrimination laws and the courts protect teachers against arbitrary and capricious acts by school officials in these cases.

5. Fail to document inappropriate or discriminatory behavior directed toward you by colleagues or school officials in your school. Timely documentation may be invaluable if a formal complaint becomes necessary.

ENDNOTES

1. 42 U.S.C. § 2000e et seq.
2. *McDonnell Douglas Corp. v. Green*, 411 U.S. 792 (1973).
3. *Furnco Construction Corp. v. Waters*, 438 U.S. 567 (1978).
4. *McDonnell Douglas* 411 U.S. 792.
5. *Todd v. Natchez-Adams School Dist.*, No. 05-60239, 2005 WL 3525596, 160 Fed. Appx. 377 (5th Cir. 2005).
6. *Schroeder v. Hamilton School District*, 282 F.3d 946 (7th Cir. 2002).
7. 20 U.S.C. § 1681 et seq. (1972).
8. 34 C.F.R. § 106.61.
9. *North Haven Board of Education v. Bell*, 456 U.S. 512 (1982).
10. 29 U.S.C. § 794 (A) (1988).
11. 29 U.S.C. § 706 (8) (B) (1988).
12. 34 C.F.R. § 104 3 (i) (2) (ii) (1991).
13. *Id.* at (10).
14. *Brown v. Board of Education*, 347 U.S. 482, 74 S. Ct. 686 (1954).
15. *Adarand Constructors, Inc. v. Pena*, 63 U.S. 4523, 115 S. Ct. at 2111 (1995).
16. *Massachusetts Board of Regents v. Murgia*, 427 U.S. 307 (1976).
17. *Cleveland Board of Education v. LaFleur*, 414 U.S. 632 (1974).
18. 29 C.F.R. § 1604, 11(a) (1991).
19. *Meritor Savings Bank v. Vinson*, 106 S. Ct. 2399 (1986).

10

Teacher Freedoms

Public school teachers do not relinquish their personal rights as a condition of accepting an employment position in the public schools. Although teachers are expected to be sensitive to the professional nature of their positions and to demonstrate a regard for the integrity of the profession, they do enjoy certain constitutional freedoms that must be respected by school authorities. Because teachers enter the profession with constitutional rights and freedoms, boards of education must establish a compelling reason to restrict these freedoms. In these instances, the burden rests with school officials to demonstrate that their actions are not arbitrary, capricious, or motivated by personal or political objectives.

The courts, in addressing conflicts involving constitutional freedoms of teachers, attempt to balance the public interest of the school district against the personal rights of each individual employee. Thus, teachers are subject to reasonable restraints, but only if a legitimate, defensible rationale is established by the school district.

SUBSTANTIVE AND PROCEDURAL CONSIDERATIONS

As stated in Chapter 3, there are two types of due process, both of which apply to teachers: procedural and substantive. *Procedural due process* means that when a teacher is deprived of life, liberty, or property, a prescribed constitutional procedure must be followed. Briefly stated, the teacher deprived must be given proper notice that he or she is to be deprived of life, liberty, or property. The teacher must be provided an opportunity to present a defense during a fair, impartial hearing. Failure to follow procedural requirements will result in a violation of the teacher's constitutional rights. *Substantive due process* means that the state must have a valid objective when it intends to deprive a teacher of life, liberty, or property, and the means used must be reasonably calculated to achieve the state's objective. Most important, both procedural and substantive requirements must be met in teacher dismissal proceedings. Many administrative decisions that were correct in substance have been overturned on appeal to higher authority simply on the grounds that procedural requirements were not met. Conversely, procedural requirements may have been met by school officials even when the evidence revealed that a valid reason did not exist that warranted depriving a teacher of his or her substantive rights. The administrative decision in this case would be overturned as well.

FREEDOM OF EXPRESSION

By virtue of the First Amendment to the Constitution, teachers are afforded rights to freedom of expression. Within limits, they enjoy the same rights and privileges regarding speech and expression as other citizens. Free speech by teachers, however, is limited to the requirement that speech does not materially disrupt the educational interest of the school district. Material disruption, for example, may involve an interference with the rights of others or may involve speech that creates a negative impact on proper school discipline and decorum. The level of protection provided teachers is generally lower in cases when the teacher speaks on matters that are personal in nature, as opposed to those that are of interest to the community.

In either case, school officials may not justifiably prohibit or penalize the teacher in any manner for exercising a constitutionally protected right, without a showing that a legitimate state interest is affected by the teacher's speech or expression. As usual, in cases when a teacher's speech is restricted, the burden of proof justifying such restriction rests with school officials. Districts have succeeded in their actions to restrict speech and discipline teachers when there was evidence that the teacher's personal speech undermined authority and adversely affected working relationships or rendered the teacher unfit to teach. In the absence of such showing, the teacher's speech is protected.

In fact, the U.S. Supreme Court addressed the application of the First Amendment in employment situations by emphasizing in *Connick v. Myers* the distinction between speech involving public concern and grievances regarding internal personnel matters. Expressions regarding public concerns, according to the High Court, receive First Amendment protections, whereas ordinary employee grievances are to be handled by the appropriate administrative body without involvement of the court.[1] In this case, the issue involved a petition circulated within an office and related to the proper functioning of the office. This type of personal speech did not receive First Amendment protection.

Speech Outside the School Environment

Teachers are afforded First Amendment rights outside the school environment. They may speak on issues that interest themselves and the community, even though the content of their speech may not be popular with school district officials.

Freedom of speech outside the school environment is well established; however, when exercising such speech, teachers must preface their comments by indicating that they are speaking as a private citizen rather than as an employee of the school board. This public disclosure is significant in establishing that the teacher's speech should not be viewed as the official position of the school district. This disclosure further reinforces the notion that the teacher possesses the same First Amendment privileges as regular citizens. For example, in *Garcetti v. Ceballos*, the U.S. Supreme Court held that the plaintiff, a district attorney, was not entitled to First Amendment protection when he criticized his employer for having passed over him for a promotion, because his public statements were made as a public employee and not as a private citizen.[2] Although teachers enjoy First Amendment rights, those rights are not without reasonable restrictions based on the nature of the position held and the positive image teachers are expected to project to students and the community. In all cases, the teacher's speech should be professional in nature and its content not designed to harm or injure another's reputation or render the teacher unfit. These standards apply whether the speech is oral or written.

A Connecticut court generated the following guidelines involving issues pertaining to freedom of expression to consider in the operation of the public schools:

1. *the impact on harmony, personal loyalty, and confidence among coworkers;*
2. *the degree of falsity of statements;*

3. *the place where speech or distribution of material occurred;*
4. *the impact on the staff and students; and*
5. *the degree to which the teacher's conduct lacked professionalism.*[3]

Generally, a teacher's rights to freedom of expression are protected. They are, however, subject to reasonable considerations regarding order, loyalty, professionalism, and overall impact on the operation of the school.

Teacher Use of Facebook and Other Social Media

Teachers enjoy rights to freedom of expression under the First Amendment. Thus, they may express their views outside the classroom like any other citizen, with the awareness that their actions often affect students they teach. The courts' view is that teachers are role models for their students and must always be sensitive to and have a reasonable regard for the nature of the profession. Consequently, teachers should exercise caution when using Facebook, Twitter, and other social media. They should refrain from messages or images that may raise questions regarding fitness to teach that may be grounds for discipline, including termination. For example, a teacher was fired for posting a picture of herself holding a glass of wine and a mug of beer and using the "b" word on Facebook. The teacher was offered an option to resign or be suspended. She elected to resign and is now seeking reinstatement to her job. Dozens of teachers have been investigated, and some have been terminated, for inappropriate interactions and relationships with students that began or were conducted on social media websites in New York City schools. Teachers should be mindful that if a particular type of behavior is inappropriate in the classroom, then it is also inappropriate on social media sites. It would be very prudent for teachers to avoid featuring students as Facebook friends. To be safe and protected, teachers should refrain from using social media to communicate with their students for noncurricular purposes.

Academic Freedom

Public school teachers are afforded a degree of academic freedom in their classrooms, based on the teacher's right to teach and the students' right to learn. Academic freedom, as a concept, originated in German universities during the nineteenth century, with the express purpose of allowing professors to teach any subject they deemed educationally appropriate.

Public school teachers, of course, are not provided the broad latitude that would allow them to introduce any subject into their teaching. Academic freedom is a limited concept in public schools. It supports the belief that the classroom should be a marketplace of ideas and that teachers should be provided freedom of inquiry, research, and discussion of various ideas and issues. Because public school teachers instruct children of tender years who are impressionable, their freedom of expression in the classroom will be affected by factors such as the grade level, age, experience, and readiness of the students to handle the content under discussion and the appropriateness of the content.

The teacher should also be certain that the subject matter introduced into classroom discussion is within the scope of the students' intellectual and social maturity levels. Public school teachers are further restrained by the requirement that content introduced into classroom discussion be related to and consistent with the teacher's certification and teaching assignment. Controversial material that is unrelated to the subject taught and that contains inappropriate content will not be supported by the courts. (Courts do not approve, but simply rule on, the appropriateness or inappropriateness of the issue at hand.)

FREEDOM OF ASSOCIATION

The First Amendment guarantees citizens the right to peaceably assemble. Within this right is included freedom of association, which grants people the right to associate with other persons of their choice without threat of punishment. Although teachers, as citizens, enjoy all these rights, they should exercise them with discretion in light of the nature and importance of their positions as public employees. Further, they should be concerned with the "role-model image" they project and the impact of their actions on impressionable young children. The Supreme Court of Iowa stated that "a teacher's conduct involving shoplifting" affected "her ability to be an effective role model for students."[4]

In the past, teachers who had been involved in organized labor organizations or educational associations received questionable treatment by their school districts. This treatment was often reflected in the form of demotions, unwarranted transfers, nonrenewal of contracts, or even terminations. The courts will no longer support this type of treatment of teachers.

Since the late 1960s, there has been a discernible trend by the courts toward providing teachers more freedom in their personal lives than they were allowed in the past. Courts now hold that teachers, including administrators, are free to join their professional organizations, assume a leadership role, campaign for membership, and negotiate with the school board on behalf of the organization without fear of reprisal. School personnel must ensure that their participation in external organizations does not in any manner reduce their effectiveness as district employees or materially or substantially disrupt the operation of the district.

School personnel may also engage in various types of political activities. They may become a candidate for public office or campaign for their favorite candidate. However, school personnel may be requested to take personal leave when they run for public office. These are permissible activities, as long as they occur after school hours and do not interfere with job effectiveness.

POLITICAL RIGHTS

The State Interest Test has been used by federal courts since the 1960s in due process and equal protection claims to determine whether a fundamental right has been violated. Therefore, state laws prohibiting public employees from participating in all types of political activities have been deemed unconstitutional. Public school teachers have the same political rights and freedoms enjoyed by all other citizens. These include, but are not limited to, running for public office, campaigning for themselves or others, developing and expounding political ideologies, and engaging in political debate. These rights, however, should be exercised with a degree of restraint inasmuch as they are not unlimited. At all times, teachers must be aware of the effect of their actions on others, especially children. Teachers should also ensure that engaging in political activities away from school does not have an adverse effect on classroom performance. Teachers must limit their political activity to acts away from the classroom and outside of the normal school day. They must further ensure that their political activity in no way interferes or infringes on their duties and responsibilities in the classroom.

In fact, the courts seem to be trending toward supporting greater political freedom for teachers, as long as the teacher exhibits prudent professional behavior, does not neglect his or her professional duties, and does not use the classroom as a political forum.

DRESS AND GROOMING

Numerous cases regarding personal appearance issues involving teachers have been litigated by the courts. School authorities generally contend that proper dress and decorum create a professional image for teachers that has a positive influence on students. Some teachers, however, contend that dress code regulations governing their appearance infringe on their rights to free expression. These teachers further believe that they should enjoy freedom, without undue restrictions, in their personal appearance.

The courts generally have agreed that school officials have the authority to regulate any aspect of a teacher's appearance that might disrupt the educational process. What has not been settled, however, is the degree of constitutional protection teachers are entitled to receive in disputes regarding dress and the type of evidence needed to invalidate restrictions on dress. To further complicate the issue, community standards and mores are also factors considered in dress and grooming rulings. School districts have traditionally restricted dress that is contrary to acceptable community norms. The courts have also established the position that school dress codes must be reasonably related to a legitimate educational purpose justified by standards of reasonableness.

Rules that restrict dress on the basis of health, safety, material and substantial disruption, or community values generally have been upheld by the courts. Rules that extend beyond these areas generally have not been supported. It seems evident that the courts recognize that teachers should be free of unreasonable restrictions governing their appearance. However, variations in standards in different communities, as well as changing societal norms, have created difficulties

The courts will not support restrictive dress and grooming codes that are unrelated to the state's interest. When challenged, the district must demonstrate that the code is related to a legitimate educational purpose and not designed to unduly and unnecessarily restrict teachers' dress. The burden of proof rests with the school district.

RIGHT TO PRIVACY

It is commonly held that teachers enjoy a measure of privacy in their personal lives. These rights should be respected to the extent that they do not violate the integrity of the community or render the teacher ineffective in performing professional duties. Within the context of privacy rights, teachers may exercise personal choices, which may range from living with a person of the opposite sex to other life-style choices. In many instances, school boards cite privacy issues involving teachers as the basis for dismissing them from their employment positions or recommending revocation of their teaching certificates. Although there does not appear to be a clear distinction between protected and unprotected lifestyle choices, the burden of proof resides with school officials to demonstrate that the teacher's lifestyle choice adversely affects the integrity of the district or that the teacher's conduct has a detrimental effect on his or her ability to relate effectively with students.

In exercising lifestyle choices, teachers must also be mindful of the professional nature of their position and the impact that their behavior has on children, who often view them as role models. For example, when a teacher engages in a private adulterous activity, it does not necessarily follow that this act intrinsically constitutes grounds for action to be taken against the teacher. Teachers are entitled to rights of privacy, as are other citizens, and these rights must be respected. Whether a school district would be successful in penalizing a teacher for private conduct would, again, be based on a district's capacity to demonstrate that the teacher's effectiveness is impaired by his or her conduct. The burden of proof clearly resides with school officials.

When a teacher has demonstrated a strong record of teaching, has been effective in relationships with students, and is respected in the community by his or her peers, it is unlikely that school officials will succeed in bringing serious actions against the teacher, such as removal from an employment position or revocation of certificate. However, if private conduct becomes highly publicized to the point that the teacher's reputation and relationships with parents or students are impaired, rendering the teacher ineffective in executing his or her duties, appropriate punitive actions taken by school officials may be supported by the courts.

In the significant 2003 ruling *Lawrence v. Texas*, the U.S. Supreme Court held that consenting adults do have a fundamental right to engage in private homosexual activity.[5] Therefore, school boards may not dismiss teachers for engaging in homosexual acts unless there is a direct connection between engaging in a homosexual act and overall fitness and effectiveness to teach based on community norms or standards. It is significant to note that many states have passed laws supporting same-sex marriages. Thus, school leaders must exercise caution in addressing same-sex relationships.

GUIDES

Teacher Freedoms

1. Teachers do not lose their constitutional rights when they enter the educational profession. Within reasonable limits, they possess the same constitutional rights as do other citizens.
2. Teachers should avoid personal attacks or libelous or slanderous statements when exercising rights of freedom of expression or expressing concerns of interest to the community.
3. Teachers should not knowingly report false information to criticize the school district's decisions or actions.
4. School officials may not penalize or otherwise discriminate against teachers for properly executing their First Amendment rights, especially regarding issues of public concern.
5. Academic freedom is a limited concept. Teachers should introduce appropriate material in the classroom related to their assigned subject matter. The classroom should never be used as a forum to advance the teacher's political or religious views.
6. Teachers may associate with whomever they wish, as long as their association or behavior does not involve illegal activity or render them unfit to perform their job functions effectively.
7. Dress, grooming, and appearance may be regulated by school boards if a compelling educational interest is demonstrated or if such codes are supported by community standards.
8. Teachers are entitled to rights of privacy and cannot be legally penalized for private, noncriminal acts that have no impact on teacher effectiveness.
9. Teachers should exercise caution in their expressions involving social media and refrain from statements that raise questions regarding fitness to teach.

RELIGIOUS FREEDOMS

The First Amendment guarantees religious freedoms to all citizens. Title VII of the Civil Rights Act of 1964 further prohibits any forms of discrimination based on religion.

Therefore, it is unlawful for a school district to deny employment, to dismiss, or to fail to renew a teacher's contract on religious grounds. Teachers, like all other citizens, possess religious rights that must be respected; but religious rights, like all other rights, are not without limits. Since teachers are public employees, and schools must remain neutral in all matters regarding religion, there are reasonable restraints that affect the exercise of religious rights in the school setting. However, teachers are completely free to fully exercise their legal religious rights outside of normal school activities.

For example, teachers may not refuse to teach certain aspects of the state-approved curriculum on the basis of religious objections or beliefs. Although the courts recognize the existence of the teacher's religious rights, they also recognize the compelling state interest in educating all children. Courts generally hold that education cannot be left to individual teachers to teach the way they please. An elementary school teacher was not supported by the U.S. Court of Appeals for the Sixth Circuit when she required students to view a videotape of her singing a religious song.[6] Teachers have no constitutional right to require others to submit to their views or to forgo a portion of their education they would otherwise be entitled to enjoy. In short, teachers cannot legally subject others, particularly students, to their religious beliefs or ideologies. They must remain neutral in their relationship with students.

Use of Religious Garb by School Personnel

The wearing of religious garb by public school teachers has created legal questions regarding rights to freedom of expression versus religious discrimination based on dress. It has been well established that public school districts may not legally deny employment opportunities to teachers because of their religious beliefs or affiliation. However, the wearing of religious garb by public school teachers raises the question whether such dress creates a sectarian influence in the classroom. Many state statutes prohibit public teachers from wearing religious garb in the classroom. Some legal experts believe that the mere presence of religious dress serves as a constant reminder of the teacher's religious orientation and could have a proselytizing effect on children.

In contrast, some public school teachers advance the argument that religious dress is a protected right regarding freedom of expression. The courts, however, have clearly established the position that the exercise of one person's rights may not infringe on the rights of others and that public interest supersedes individual interests. Further, prohibiting a teacher from wearing religious dress does not adversely affect the teacher's belief system. It merely means that teachers cannot exercise their beliefs through dress during the period of the day in which they are employed. There is no interference outside of the school day. Thus, a teacher is free to fully exercise religious rights and freedoms outside normal hours of employment.

The courts have not reached consensus on this issue. Unless prohibited by state statute, district policy, or court decisions in certain jurisdictions, teachers may wear religious garb including clothing and jewelry. The clothing should convey that the teacher adheres to a particular faith and not be worn to proselytize. The obvious difficulty in wearing religious garb is that it may invite questions by students, and the establishment clause prohibits teachers from discussing their religious beliefs or affiliations in the classroom. Religious garb may include items such as Christian crosses, Jewish yarmulkes, Abaya or Sikh turbans, Muslim hijabs or headscarves, and the like. Dress and symbols should reflect the teacher's faith rather than a particular religion. In the absence of state statutes, the courts have been quite consistent in allowing school leaders to regulate teachers' religious clothing based on the First Amendment's establishment clause.

TITLE VII: RELIGIOUS DISCRIMINATION

Title VII addresses any forms of religious discrimination regarding employment. *Religion* is defined under Title VII to include "all aspects of religious observances, practices and beliefs."[7] This section also requires that an employer, including a school board, make reasonable accommodations to the employee's religion, unless the employer can demonstrate the inability to do so on the basis of undue hardship. Furthermore, school officials must respect and, whenever possible, make allowances for teachers' religious observances if such observances do not substantially disrupt the educational process. Accommodations may include granting personal leave to attend a religious convention or to observe a religious holiday. Unless there is evidence of undue hardship, reasonable accommodation must be provided. If requests are deemed excessive, resulting in considerable disruption to children's education, a denial would be appropriate.

Whenever school officials deny excessive leave for religious purposes, the burden of proof rests with the teacher to demonstrate that the officials' decision involved the denial of certain religious freedoms. If the teacher is able to demonstrate discriminatory intent, then the burden shifts to school officials to show a legitimate state interest, such as a disruption of education services to children. The Equal Employment Opportunity Commission (EEOC) or a court would be hard pressed to challenge a legitimate state interest involving the proper education of children.

GUIDES

Title VII: Religious Discrimination

1. The religious rights of teachers must be respected, as long as they do not violate the establishment clause of the First Amendment by creating excessive entanglement in the school.
2. School officials must make reasonable accommodations for teachers regarding observance of special religious holidays, as long as such accommodations are not deemed excessive or disruptive to the educational process.
3. Teachers should not be coerced to participate in nonacademic ceremonies or activities that violate their religious beliefs or convictions.
4. Teachers may be requested to present documented evidence that a religious belief or right has been violated in cases involving discipline of teachers for activities carried out in the performance of their nonacademic duties.
5. No form of religious discrimination may be used in decisions regarding employment, promotion, salary increments, transfers, demotions, or dismissals.
6. Unless restricted by state statute, district policy, or court decisions, teachers may wear certain types of religious clothing subject to reasonable restrictions by school officials.

PRACTICAL TIPS

Do:

1. Make certain that your public expressions on controversial community issues are not viewed as statements endorsed by your school district but, rather, are

understood to be statements by you as a private citizen. Disclosures of this nature protect your rights to freedom of expression.

2. Ensure that your public statements reflect public concern rather than a personal grievance. Personal grievances that are aired publicly will not likely receive First Amendment protection.

3. Make certain that political activities are conducted away from school, involve no school resources, and do not interfere with professional duties and responsibilities.

4. Remember that teachers' dress should conform to high standards of professionalism and in some instances community expectations. Professionalism in some communities is linked with manner of dress.

5. Exercise your personal rights in ways that account for the sensitive nature of your position as a role model for students and the integrity of the teaching profession as a whole.

Do not:

1. Assume that teachers have the right to determine the content of the school's instructional program under the concept of academic freedom. Teachers must follow the prescribed course of study in the classroom.

2. Use the classroom as a forum to proselytize students and to express views on unauthorized topics in the classroom. This practice may violate school or district policy and may result in serious disciplinary sanctions.

3. Ignore the culture and mores of the community in which your school is located. Community norms and ethics affect, to a degree, what is considered acceptable and unacceptable teacher behavior outside of the school environment.

4. Forget that boards of education have an obligation to balance a teacher's privacy rights against the district's legitimate interest in protecting the welfare of students. The school board must ensure that protecting a teacher's privacy rights does not have an adverse effect on the teacher's job performance or proves to be detrimental to students.

5. Participate in any activity that may create embarrassment for your school district or render you unfit because of the nature of the activity and its impact on the district.

ENDNOTES

1. *Connick v. Myers*, 461 U.S. 138 (1983).
2. *Garcetti v. Ceballos*, 547 U.S. 410 (2006).
3. *Gilbertson v. McAlister*, 403 F. Supp. 1 (D. Conn. 1975).
4. *Board of Directors of Lawton-Bronson v. Davies*, 489 N.W.2d 19 S. Ct. of Iowa (1992).
5. *Lawrence v. Texas*, 123 S. Ct. 2472 (2003).
6. *DeNooyer v. Livonia Public Schools*, 12 F.3d 211 (6th Circuit 1993), *cert. denied*, 114 S. Ct. 1540 (1994).
7. 42 U.S.C. § 2000e (2).

11

Tenure, Dismissal, and Collective Negotiations

TENURE

Tenure in public schools is prescribed by state statute. Although they vary among states, tenure laws are designed to protect capable teachers. The *tenure contract* is primarily designed to provide a measure of security for teachers and to ensure that they are protected from arbitrary and capricious treatment by school officials. Tenure also is viewed as a means of providing a degree of permanency in the teaching force, from which students ultimately benefit. Any teacher who earns tenure or continuing service status also acquires a property right, or a legitimate claim, to the teaching position. Once a property right is acquired, the teacher may be dismissed only for cause. Tenure does not guarantee continued employment but does ensure that certified school personnel may not arbitrarily be removed from their employment positions without due process of law. The intended purpose of tenure laws has been described by the courts. One court described it in this manner:

> While tenure provisions . . . protect teachers in their
> positions from political or arbitrary interference,
> they are not intended to preclude dismissal where the
> conduct is detrimental to the efficient operation and
> administration of the schools of the district. . . . Its
> objective is to improve the school system by assuring
> teachers of experience and ability to continuous service
> based upon merit by protecting them against dismissal
> for reasons that are political, partisan or capricious.[1]

This protection insulates teachers from special interest groups and political factions, and thereby enables them to perform their professional duties without undue interference. Thus, the education system is improved and students derive the benefits of quality education.

Acquisition of Tenure

In a number of states, tenure may be attained only after the teacher has successfully completed 3 successive years in the same district during the probationary period and has received an offer for reemployment for the succeeding year. The *probationary period* is a period during which the nontenured teacher is seeking tenure. School boards are provided broad latitude in determining whether tenure should be granted. During the probationary period, a teacher may be denied renewal at the end of the contract year without cause, or dismissed during the contract year with cause. In the latter case, the teacher must be afforded full due process rights. There is no requirement for due process provisions in cases involving nonrenewal unless the teacher is able to demonstrate that nonrenewal was based purely on personal or political motives, or motivated by arbitrary and capricious actions involving infringement on constitutional rights. This is usually a difficult burden of proof to meet but one that, ultimately, rests with the probationary teacher.

Because state laws prescribe that certain substantive and procedural requirements be met regarding tenure, it is essential that school districts adhere to these requirements. (See Chapter 9 for a discussion of substantive and procedural issues.) Generally, state statutes specify a date by which a probationary teacher must be informed that employment opportunities will no longer be available for the succeeding year. This notice informing the teacher of nonrenewal is normally forwarded to the teacher by certified or registered mail to the latest known address on or before a specified date. If the district fails to meet this requirement, the teacher may have gained employment for the following year. When a teacher has completed 3 consecutive years in the same district and does not receive timely notice of nonrenewal, the teacher may acquire tenure by *default*. In most states, no reasons need be given for nonrenewal of a probationary teacher's contract.

In sum, nontenured status involves

- no expectation for employment beyond the contracted year,
- no right to be provided reasons for nonrenewal,
- no right to due process, and
- no hearing.

These conditions are valid unless the nontenured teacher produces evidence that a liberty or property right exists, in which case due process must be provided. A *liberty right* exists when damaging statements that may limit the teacher's range of future employment opportunities are communicated by the school board. A *property right* exists only if the nontenured teacher's contract is canceled during the contract or school year.

Nonrenewal

The primary reason that due process does not apply to probationary status centers around a limited property interest. During the probationary period, the teacher typically is offered a 1-year contract that is renewable each year if the school board elects to renew. The probationary teacher then has a property right for only the duration of each 1-year contract. When the contract period ends each year, the teacher loses the inherent property right because both the teacher and the district have met their contractual obligations to each other. Due process and cause are necessary only if there is evidence that a property interest continues to exist. A property interest does not exist if there is no legal contract in force. However, as stated previously, if a district decides to dismiss a probationary teacher during the contract period, then full due process provisions are required, including notice, cause, and a formal hearing, because the teacher has a property right for the duration of the contract year.

GUIDES

Tenure

1. Teachers are entitled to fundamental fairness, irrespective of tenure status.
2. Tenure is not designed to protect teachers who are inept or ineffective but, rather, those who are competent and effective.
3. Tenured teachers may be legally dismissed only for specified reasons that are based on objective and documented evidence.
4. Due process procedural safeguards, as established by state statutes, should be followed to ensure that dismissal decisions are legally defensible.
5. Nonrenewal of a nontenured teacher's contract does not generally require due process or reasons, unless there is an alleged constitutional violation a liberty or property right is involved.

Teacher Evaluation

The primary purpose of teacher evaluation is to assess a teacher's effectiveness and to provide guidance and direction for improvement. Most school districts have well-developed policies and procedures, along with prescribed evaluation forms, that guide the evaluation process. Ideally, the teacher should be informed of a proposed evaluation. Evaluations should be administered systematically. The teacher's performance should be documented, including strengths and areas in need of improvement. To the greatest degree possible, documentation should be quantified. Evaluation scores should be compared with predetermined standards to determine teacher effectiveness. Ideally, teacher effectiveness should be a measure of student learning outcomes. A thorough improvement plan should be developed that is based on evaluation results, with a reasonable time frame provided for the teacher to meet expected performance standards. Administrative assistance and support should be provided during that period. If evaluations are used for any purpose other than the improvement of performance, the teacher should be informed of such use.

There should be provisions for the teacher to rebut any evaluation he or she thinks is unfair. The teacher should also be provided an opportunity to seek another evaluation by an alternative supervisor if the teacher believes that the previous evaluation was inaccurate or extraordinarily subjective. Fundamental fairness should guide the evaluation process. Courts are generally reluctant to substitute their judgment in cases involving teacher evaluation. However, they will address issues involving procedural matters with respect to fundamental fairness.

GUIDES

Teacher Evaluation

1. Evaluation criteria should be communicated to teachers and applied fairly and consistently.
2. If evaluations are used for any purpose other than improvement of performance, the teacher should be informed of their use.
3. Administrative support is an essential component of the teacher performance improvement plan.

FINANCIAL EXIGENCY (ELIMINATION OF POSITIONS)

Financial exigency occurs when the district faces a bona fide reduction in its budget that results in the need to eliminate certain employment positions. Positions may also be eliminated when the district encounters reductions in student enrollment. The courts will generally support districts that demonstrate the need to reduce their teaching force by a practice commonly called *reduction in force* (RIF) when there is evidence that a legitimate financial problem exists. Obviously, districts should implement RIF policies and procedures that ensure that substantive and procedural due process requirements involving school personnel are met. Generally, the due process expectations are not as stringent in RIF cases, because dismissal decisions are based primarily on financial concerns as opposed to personal or performance issues. In supporting financial exigency, the courts usually require school districts to demonstrate the following:

1. A bona fide financial crisis exists.
2. A rational relationship between the benefits derived from dismissal and the alleviation of the financial crisis exists.
3. A fair and uniform set of due process procedures is followed in dismissal decisions.

School districts attempt to use objective criteria in building their RIF policies. Districts generally use the following criteria in making RIF decisions:

1. subject matter needs,
2. teachers' length of experience (seniority) in the district,
3. teachers' length of experience in the teaching profession,
4. highest degree or certificate earned,
5. length of time in which the degree or certificate has been held,
6. subject matter qualifications, and
7. teaching performance.

School districts typically attempt to reduce staff through voluntary retirements, resignations, leaves of absence, and transfers. These areas should normally be addressed before action is taken to implement a RIF plan. Teachers should review specific RIF policies and procedures, because these vary among districts.

GUIDES

Financial Exigency

1. All employees affected by a RIF must be afforded full due process provisions.
2. The burden of demonstrating bona fide financial exigency rests with the board of education.

3. School districts may not use financial exigency as a means to remove a teacher if the removal is in violation of the teacher's exercised, constitutionally protected right.
4. Seniority and job performance should receive priority in RIF decisions.
5. School district policy and/or state statutes should be followed judiciously in implementing RIF policies.

DISMISSAL FOR CAUSE

Dismissing a teacher for cause is a serious matter, because the teacher has an inherent property right to hold the employment position. State statutes prescribe permissible legal grounds on which dismissal shall be based. In these cases, the burden of proof resides with the board of education to show cause based on a preponderance of evidence. The obvious benefit of tenure to the teacher is that he or she cannot be dismissed without a formal hearing and the presentation of sufficient evidence to meet statutory requirements, which assures the teacher that procedural and substantive due process requirements have been met.

Tenure laws include grounds for dismissal in virtually all states. Although these grounds vary among states, they normally include incompetency; insubordination; neglect of duty; immorality; a justifiable decrease in the number of teaching positions, or financial exigency; and a statement indicating *other good and just cause.* The latter phrase provides the board with broader latitude to address other grounds that may not be specified by statute. A board of education may dismiss a teacher for almost any reason, as long as the reason is valid and meets due process requirements.

Incompetency

One of the more frequently used grounds for dismissal involves charges of incompetency. *Incompetency* is a vague term in many respects. In some states, incompetency is used as the sole grounds for dismissal for almost any reason. Most commonly, incompetency refers to inefficiency, a lack of skill, inadequate knowledge of subject matter, inability or unwillingness to teach the curriculum, failure to work effectively with colleagues and parents, failure to maintain discipline, mismanagement of the classroom, and attitudinal deficiencies. Because the court views the teaching certificate as prima facie proof of competency, the burden of proof challenging a teacher's competency rests with the school board. The competent teacher is generally viewed as a person who has the knowledge, skills, and intelligence of the average or ordinary teacher.

If charges of incompetency are brought against a teacher, these charges should be preceded by systematic evaluations and documentation of the teacher's performance, as well as a thoroughly developed teacher improvement plan. Proper documentation and a reasonable time frame designed to allow the teacher to meet expected performance standards are critical to sustaining a charge of incompetence, should such a charge become necessary.

Insubordination

Insubordination is generally viewed as the willful failure or inability to obey a reasonable and valid administrative directive. In most cases, there is a discernible pattern in the teacher's behavior that reveals that the teacher has been insubordinate. However, sometimes a single serious violation may form the basis for a charge of insubordination. In most cases involving insubordination, the teacher has been given explicit warning regarding the undesirable conduct and has failed to heed the warning. In such cases, charges of insubordination are usually sustained.

For insubordination charges to be upheld there must be documented evidence of the alleged misconduct, with further evidence that the administrative order or directive was valid. Insubordination charges are more likely to succeed when they are linked with teaching performance or related academic issues. If the evidence reveals that the directive or administrative order was biased against the teacher or was unreasonable, then insubordination charges will be difficult to defend. Also, there should be no evidence that the order or rules violated the teacher's personal rights.

Neglect of Duty

Neglect of duty occurs when a teacher fails to execute assigned duties. Neglect may be intentional or unintentional, depending on the nature of the ineffective performance. One court defined *neglect of duty* as the failure to carry out professional obligations and responsibilities in connection with classroom or other school-sponsored activities.[2] Another court held that neglect of duty involving performance is not measured against a standard of perfection but must be measured against the standard required of others performing the same or similar duties.[3]

Immorality

Immorality is cited in relevant state statutes as grounds for dismissal and involves conduct that violates the ethics of a particular community. Some state laws refer to immorality as *unfitness to teach*, or behavior that sets a poor example for students and violates moral integrity. One court held that the conduct in question not only must be immoral under the particular community standards test but also must be found to impair the teacher's ability to teach.[4] This latter statement seems to reflect the consensus of court decisions regarding issues of immorality in that there must be evidence that the conduct in question impairs the teacher's effectiveness in the classroom.

Teachers and Ethical Behavior

Public school teachers are considered role models by the courts owing to their influence on students, particularly very young ones. Consequently, teachers should always adhere to high standards of professional conduct in and outside the classroom. As the U.S. Supreme Court ruled in *Ambach v. Norwick*:

> *Within the public school system, teachers play a critical part in developing students' attitude toward government and understanding of the role of citizens in our society. . . . Further, a teacher serves as a role model for his/her students exerting a subtle but important influence over their perception and values.*[5]

A teacher's action can have a great impact and influence on his or her students. Therefore, teachers should possess sound moral and ethical values. They must understand the moral and ethical complexities of their role and ensure that their actions reflect high standards of ethical behavior. The National Education Association (NEA) has formulated a code of ethics that involves commitment to students and commitment to the profession with sound principles that influence a teacher's behavior under each category. Teachers must always be sensitive to and have a high regard for the nature of their positions and the impact of their behavior on students.

Conduct Involving Morality

Public school teachers serve in highly visible and significant positions, and they often exert an important influence on the views of students and the formation of students' values. Because of teachers' unique roles, there is an expectation that a teacher's character and personal conduct be on a higher plane than that of the average citizen, who does not interact with students on a daily basis.

One of the most-quoted definitions of the term *immorality*, established by the Supreme Court of Pennsylvania in 1939, is "a course of conduct which offends the morals of a community and is a bad example to the youth whose ideals a teacher is supposed to foster and elevate."[6]

Sexual Advances Toward Students

Courts have left little doubt that they will deal firmly with teachers in matters involving improper sexual conduct toward students. The courts support the general view that teaching is an exemplary professional activity, and those who teach should exhibit behavior that is above reproach in their dealings with students. Many state statutes include provisions that require teachers to impress the principles of truth, morality, temperance, and humanity on the minds of their students. These are very high standards that teachers are expected to meet in their professional roles. Given the position of the courts and the provisions in many state laws governing teacher conduct, it is not surprising to find courts consistently upholding the positions of school districts that produce evidence that a teacher has engaged in unlawful sexual involvement with students.

For example, a male teacher was dismissed for immoral conduct after he placed his hands inside the jeans of a student in the area of her buttocks and on other occasions squeezed the breast of a female student. The court determined the teacher's conduct to be grossly inappropriate.[7]

In another case, a male teacher was dismissed for professional misconduct after he tickled and touched female students on various parts of their bodies while on a field trip. He also touched them between the legs, and was found lying on a bed with one of the female students, watching television. The court determined that his activities were sufficient to sustain charges of unfitness to teach.[8]

A tenured art teacher was dismissed for immoral conduct after he placed his hands on female students, giving back rubs that led to further sexual contact. Evidence was also presented that he had engaged in sexual intercourse with two students at various places in the building.[9] A female teacher resigned and surrendered her teaching certificate after a substitute teacher discovered a note from a student to the teacher, threatening to expose their personal relationship if she did not comply with certain demands.[10]

Other acts that have fallen under the category of immorality include public sexual activity, unprofessional conduct, and criminal activity involving moral turpitude. Any act or behavior that substantially interferes with the education of children and has a direct impact on the teacher's fitness to teach can usually form the basis of an immorality charge. One fundamental determination courts seek to make is whether the teacher's alleged conduct adversely affected teaching performance and effectiveness. The finding, in many cases, will determine whether a teacher should be dismissed.

GUIDES

Dismissal for Cause

1. School officials should avoid any actions regarding evaluation for dismissal that may be viewed by the affected teacher as harassment or intimidation.
2. School officials should know their state's statutory definition of insubordination and ensure that cases involving insubordination are well documented. Professional disagreements between superiors and subordinates do not normally constitute insubordination.
3. Conviction of a felony or a series of misdemeanors may form grounds for dismissal and revocation of the teaching certificate.
4. Sexual misconduct by school personnel involving students will almost always result in dismissal and, possibly, criminal charges.
5. Teachers should adhere to high standards of ethical behavior based on their unique influence on students.

Good or Just Cause

Just cause is designed to provide the district broader latitude in dismissing teachers for causes not specifically identified in state statutes. It is not designed to allow the district to dismiss a teacher for personal, political, arbitrary, or capricious reasons. The same due process provisions must be met under this category as would be met under the more specific causes for dismissal. As long as the board can justify its actions as being fair and reasonably related to a legitimate state interest, there should be no challenge by the courts. Just cause is not a category used frequently by school districts. Most tend to rely on the more specific causes previously identified.

Good or just cause may be used to bring dismissal charges against a teacher, particularly when there is a showing that performance and effectiveness are impaired and when a question of fitness to teach arises as a major concern. Because this category is covered by many state statutes, school districts may use it as long as due process provisions are met. As with all charges, the burden of proof rests with school officials.

GUIDES

Good or Just Cause

1. Good or just cause provisions should not be used to attempt to justify an arbitrary dismissal of a teacher from an employment position.
2. Good or just cause should never be motivated by a desire to suppress the exercise of constitutionally protected rights of teachers, such as free speech and free association.
3. The burden of proof should always reside with school officials to demonstrate that just cause is valid.

COLLECTIVE BARGAINING

Collective bargaining has grown in popularity and appeal in public education. Although the process has always provoked controversy, many educators view collective bargaining as a mechanism to achieve a greater role in management and operation of public schools. Because many of the issues involving collective bargaining center on rights of employees and terms and conditions of employment, by its very nature collective bargaining sometimes evokes conflict and adversarial relationships between school boards and union representatives.

It is well recognized that collective bargaining has not always enjoyed the popularity it enjoys today. In fact, it did not gain legal protection in the private sector until the early 1930s. The concept in the public sector evolved very slowly, owing primarily to the belief in and acceptance of governmental sovereignty. As agents of the state, public schools exerted almost complete control of school operations, as well as terms and conditions of employment, consistent with their state's statutory mandates and local district policies. The prevailing view among state lawmakers was that this sovereign power should not be abrogated.

Collective bargaining gradually emerged in the public sector in the late 1940s when Wisconsin became one of the first states to enact legislation allowing bargaining to occur. However, it was not until the 1960s that teachers launched a major effort to gain a greater level of involvement in the administration and operation of their schools. Most states currently permit some form of bargaining between teachers and school boards. These agreements may vary from required bargaining to some form of meet-and-confer provision.

Irrespective of these variations, the basic intent of collective bargaining is to empower teachers and to share power between teachers and school boards. Obviously, some states are more liberal than others in deciding which items are negotiable. For example, arbitration is mandated in some states but prohibited in others. In any case, the primary objective is to create conditions in which school employees are afforded the opportunity to affiliate with a union without fear of reprisal for their participation. One common element found in most state statutes is a *good faith* requirement imposed on employers, which implies that the employers must bargain with the recognized bargaining unit with the sincere intent of reaching a reasonable agreement. In fact, this good faith provision affects both parties during the bargaining process.

Private Sector Versus Public Sector Bargaining

There are obvious differences between private and public sector bargaining. One of the most notable differences is that private sector employees do not enjoy constitutional protections as do public sector employees. Public sector employees are afforded equal-rights protection under due process, as well as the protection of certain rights enacted by state statutes.

Private sector rights were severely restructured in 1947 by amendment to the National Labor Relations Act (NLRA), which had been passed in 1935 to support collective bargaining in an effort to improve management and labor relations. The National Labor Relations Board (NLRB) was formed during this time to remedy unfair labor practices. The amendments to the NLRA imposed limitations on various union practices after widespread evidence of union corruption surfaced. The amended version resulted in the Labor Management Relations Act, commonly called the Taft-Hartley Act. This act was subsequently amended in 1959 by the Labor Management Reporting and Disclosure Act (LMRDA), which provided protection to private sector employees who faced various forms of union abuse. It also invoked penalties for misappropriation of union funds.

Another significant difference is that, in many instances, public school teachers are not permitted to strike. Proponents of public sector negotiations view this restriction as a real limitation, in the sense that bargaining strength is weakened in the capacity to reject the terms and conditions offered during the negotiation process. In the private sector, rejection of an offer is most often followed by a strike when an impasse occurs. In states where strikes are prohibited by law, penalties ranging from loss of salary to dismissal for teachers and heavy fines for union officials are imposed. When an impasse occurs, public sector bargaining is also affected by state and local budget restraints. Because funding is determined by state legislatures and dependent on tax projections and revenue, regulations regarding salary issues are limited by state appropriations to education, irrespective of bargaining agreements.

State Involvement

A number of states have passed permissive legislation to aid recognized union organizations. Some states support an *agency shop* measure, which stipulates that a teacher must pay dues or some form of service charge to the union if the teacher is not a member of the recognized bargaining unit. A few state laws make union affiliation mandatory for teachers as a condition to continuing their employment. An organization that executes such an agreement is commonly referred to as a *union shop*. Other states require teachers to affiliate with the recognized bargaining unit when they apply for a teaching position. This arrangement is commonly referred to as a *closed shop*. Still other states have enacted legislation to protect employees from harassment by employers and union officials if the employees elect not to affiliate with the bargaining unit. When a bargaining unit is granted the exclusive right to represent employees, it must do so on a fair and equitable basis, irrespective of whether the employee is a member or not. In most cases state law requires the union to do this.

Figure 11.1 delineates collective bargaining status for public employees. Some states cover all workers, others cover selected workers, and some states cover no workers.

Scope of Collective Bargaining

State laws vary regarding issues deemed negotiable, and these are normally grouped under the categories mandatory, permissive, and illegal. Issues pertaining to working conditions such as length of the work day, school teaching workload,

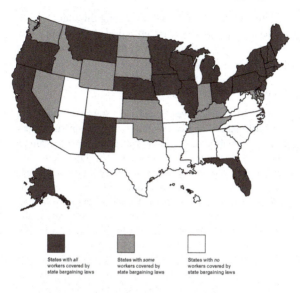

FIGURE 11.1 Collective bargaining status for public employees.
Source: U.S. Department of Labor, www.dol.gov

extra duty assignments, and leaves of absence and other fringe benefits are almost always considered mandatory, which means that bargaining is mandatory. Permissive subjects are generally based on common agreement between the parties and do not constitute a breach of duty to bargain in good faith. Issues involving personnel recruitment, selection, and induction are considered administrative prerogatives not subject to mandatory negotiations. Because these areas vary among states, there is no clear distinction among these areas.

In areas involving mandatory bargaining, school boards are required to operate in good faith bargaining. As previously indicated, state statutes establish the framework regarding the scope of collective negotiations in public schools. Several basic issues emerge in relation to negotiation agreements. These normally cover areas that a school board may negotiate, as well as those it shall not negotiate. Also covered are issues that must be negotiated until agreement is reached by both parties. Issues that are not mandatory or permissive in some states are negotiated between the teacher's union and the school board. They include areas such as teacher's planning periods, changes in the length of class periods, nonteaching assignments, sick leave banks, and academic policies.

Although there are variations among the states regarding negotiable items, there is a great deal of consistency with respect to managerial prerogatives that must remain under the purview of the school board.[11]

Impasse and Bargaining

In a fairly recent development, the states of Ohio and Wisconsin passed regulations that severely limit employees' ability to bargain collectively. Both states prohibit bargaining over health coverage and pensions. The Ohio law gives city councils and school boards the freedom to unilaterally impose their side's final contract offer when management and the union reach an impasse. The Wisconsin law bars the state from deducting workers' dues from their paychecks. It also requires an annual vote to determine whether government workers wish to maintain a union. Both states allow government employees to opt out of paying union dues or fees.

Often, the parties involved in negotiations fail to reach an agreement, and it becomes obvious that no further progress is possible toward resolution; that is, an *impasse* is reached. The regular negotiation process calls for a series of options designed to resolve the dispute:

1. *Mediation* occurs when a neutral party is engaged to assist both parties in reaching objective solutions to the dispute at hand. The mediation is normally chosen by common agreement between parties. If mediation fails, another option is to engage a fact-finder.
2. A *fact-finder* is a third party who attempts to analyze facts and determine where compromise might occur. The fact-finder offers solutions that are not binding on either party. If the fact-finding process fails to resolve the dispute, the final step is arbitration.
3. *Arbitration* occurs when a third party performs similar functions to those performed by the fact-finder. If the arbitration is *binding*, then the recommended resolution to the dispute is mandatory for both parties.

Workers' Compensation

Teachers are protected by workers' compensation in most states when they are injured during the course of performing their professional duties. The theory supporting workers' compensation is that the employing agency should assume responsibility for injuries suffered by employees during the conduct of the agency's business. Workers' compensation does not normally apply when an employee is willfully or wrongfully injured by the employer or a colleague.

The injured employee does not need to prove that any injury resulted from a certain incident but only that the injury is work related. In recent years, the courts have permitted greater flexibility and latitude, allowing compensation for a job-related injury that developed over time. For example, a teacher might incur an injury over time by lifting heavy equipment or performing routine tasks such as rearranging furniture in the classroom. In some instances, an employee is covered by workers' compensation if a work condition or an incident at work aggravates a preexisting condition. In all cases, evidence must support that the injury was a result of the execution of professional duties and responsibilities. It is very difficult in most instances to receive coverage for psychological or mental illness, unless the employee can adequately demonstrate that he or she endured an unusually stressful, unavoidable work environment. An employee will not normally prevail in cases of self-induced stress that develops from ineffectiveness in performing expected job duties and responsibilities. Most states have explicit processes and procedures that employees must follow to receive workers' compensation, including a specified time in which an injury covered by state statutes must be reported. Virtually every state has an agency that administers the program. As a last resort, employees may turn to the courts if they are denied workers' compensation benefits, once they have exhausted all other possibilities in following the state's procedures.

GUIDES

Collective Bargaining

1. The collective negotiations process should always be guided by a good faith effort involving both parties—school boards and union officials.
2. School boards should not negotiate items over which they have no legal authority, such as state salary increases and employment of personnel, unless there is express statutory authority to do so.
3. Any sustained action taken by striking teachers that may disrupt educational opportunities for students will not likely receive court support.

4. Constitutionally protected rights and freedoms of teachers should not be impaired by collective bargaining agreements.
5. Teachers are protected by workers' compensation when they sustain job-related injuries.

PRACTICAL TIPS

Do:

1. Understand the criteria or standards for attaining tenure in your state and make every effort to meet those expectations. Annual evaluation results and performance improvement plans will greatly influence the acquisition of tenure.
2. Learn the statutory reasons for dismissal in your state. This knowledge should assist you as a teacher in every phase of executing your daily responsibilities.
3. Understand that tenure ensures that a tenured teacher will be provided notice of charges and an opportunity to respond to specific charges if dismissal is contemplated. Tenure does not guarantee that a tenured teacher cannot be dismissed. It merely ensures that a valid reason must exist for the contemplated dismissal, consistent with due process.
4. Be aware that awarding tenure is not required of a school board. It does not occur automatically and must be earned on the basis of your performance and the district's needs.

Do not:

1. Expect tenure laws to provide protection against poor performance. Tenure laws are designed to protect only tenured teachers who are effective.
2. Expect due process in nonrenewal decisions, unless the nonrenewal is prescribed by state law or there is evidence that a nonrenewal decision damaged your reputation or future employment opportunities. The burden of proof rests with the teacher.
3. Refuse to follow a school policy or regulation even if you disagree with its application. In cases of disagreement, follow prescribed procedures to address the issue.
4. Engage in any behavior that fits the statutory reasons for dismissal in your state. You should become familiar with statutory causes for dismissal and utilize appropriate measures to avoid situations that may lead to dismissal.

ENDNOTES

1. *Pickering v. Board of Education*, 225 N.E.2d, 16 (Ill. 1967).

2. *Blaine v. Moffat County School District Region No. 1*, 748 P.2d 1280 (Colo. 1998).

3. *Sanders v. Board of Education of South Sioux Community School District No. 11*, 263 N.W.2d 461, Neb. (1978).

4. *Thompson v. Southwest School District*, 483 F. Supp. 1170 (Mo. 1980).

5. *Ambach v. Norwick*, 441 U.S. 68, 78–79 (1978).

6. *Horosko v. Mt. Pleasant School District*, 335 Pa. 369 6 A.2d 866 (1939), *cert. denied*, 308 U.S. 553 (1939).

7. *Fadler v. Illinois State Board of Education*, 506 N.E.2d 640 (Ill. Ct. App. 1987).

8. *Weissman v. Board of Education of Jefferson County School District No. R-1*, 190 Colo. 414, 547 P.2d 1267 (1976).

9. *Johnson v. Beaverhead City High School District*, 236 Mont. 532, 771 P.2d 137 (1989).

10. *Sauls v. Pierce County Sch. Dist.*, 399 F.3d. 1279, 1285 (11th Cir. 2005).

11. *Rochester Area School District v. Rochester Education Association*, No. 2915 C.D. 1999 (Pa. Commw. Ct. 2000).

Constitution of the United States

THE PREAMBLE

We the People of the United States, in Order to form a more perfect Union, establish Justice, insure domestic Tranquility, provide for the common defence, promote the general Welfare, and secure the Blessings of Liberty to ourselves and our Posterity, do ordain and establish this Constitution for the United States of America.

See www.usconstitution.net/const.html for the full text of the U.S. Constitution.

Summary of Relevant Federal Statutes

CIVIL RIGHTS ACT OF 1871—42 U.S.C. § 1983

Section 1983 provides that "Every person who, under color of any statute, ordinance, regulation, custom or usage, of any State or Territory, subjects, or causes to be subjected, any citizen of the United States or other person within the jurisdiction thereof to the *deprivation of any rights*, privileges or immunities *secured by the Constitution and laws*, shall be liable to the party injured in an action at law, suit in equity, or other proper proceeding for redress."

CIVIL RIGHTS ACT OF 1964 TITLE VII (SELECTED PARTS) 42 U.S.C.A. § 2000E–2

EQUAL EMPLOYMENT OPPORTUNITIES
§ 2000e–2. Unlawful employment practices

Employer Practices

(a) It shall be an unlawful employment practice for an employer

(1) to fail or refuse to hire or to discharge any individual, or otherwise to discriminate against any individual with respect to his compensation, terms, conditions, or privileges of employment, because of such individual's race, color, religion, sex, or national origin; or

(2) to limit, segregate, or classify his employees or applicants for employment in any way which would deprive or tend to deprive any individual of employment opportunities or otherwise adversely affect his status as an employee, because of such individual's race, color, religion, sex, or national origin.

Education Amendments of 1972, Title IX–20 U.S.C. § 1681

Section 901 of Title IX provides, in part, that

(A) *No person . . .* shall, on the basis of *sex*, be excluded from participation in, be denied the benefits of, or be subjected to discrimination under any *education program* or activity *receiving Federal financial assistance,* except that:

(1) in regard to admissions . . .

(2) this section *shall not apply* to an educational institution which is controlled by a religious organization if the application . . . would not be consistent *with the religious tenets* of such organization. . . .

Title IX regulations provide, in part, for "[n]ondiscrimination on the Basis of Sex in Education Programs and Activities; Receiving or Benefiting from Federal Financial Assistance," 34 C.F.R. § 106.1–106.71.

FAMILY RIGHTS AND PRIVACY ACT (BUCKLEY AMENDMENT) (SELECTED PARTS) 20 U.S.C.A. § 1232G

§ 1232g. Family educational and privacy rights

Conditions for availability of funds to educational agencies or institutions; inspection and review of education records; specific information to be made available; procedure for access to education records; reasonableness of time for such access; hearings; written explanations by parents; definitions.

(a)(1)(A) No funds shall be made available under any applicable program to any educational agency or institution which has a policy of denying, or which effectively prevents, the parents of students who are or have been in attendance at a school of such agency or at such institution, as the case may be, the right to inspect and review the education records of their children. If any material or document in the education record of a student includes information on more than one student, the parents of one of such students shall have the right to inspect and review only such part of such material or document as relates to such student or to be informed of the specific information contained in such part of such material. Each educational agency or institution shall establish appropriate procedures for the granting of a request by parents for access to the education records of their children within a reasonable period of time, but in no case more than forty-five days after the request has been made . . .

(2) No funds shall be made available under any applicable program to any educational agency or institution unless the parents of students who are or have been in attendance at a school of such agency or at such institution are provided an opportunity for a hearing by such agency or institution, in accordance with regulations of the Secretary, to challenge the content of such student's education records, in order to insure that the records are not inaccurate, misleading, or otherwise in violation of the privacy or other rights of students, and to provide an opportunity for the correction or deletion of any such inaccurate, misleading, or otherwise inappropriate data contained therein and to insert into such records a written explanation of the parents respecting the content of such records. . . .

AMERICANS WITH DISABILITIES ACT OF 1990 (SELECTED PARTS), PUBLIC LAW 101–336, 42 U.S.C. § 12101

Title I—Employment

§ 101. Definitions

As used in this title, the following definitions apply:

(1) Commission—The term *Commission* means the Equal Employment Opportunity Commission established by section 705 of the Civil Rights Act of 1964 (42 U.S.C. 2000e–4).

(2) Covered entity—The term *covered entity* means an employer, employment agency, labor organization, or joint labor–management committee.

(3) Direct threat—The term *direct threat* means a significant risk to the health or safety of others that cannot be eliminated by reasonable accommodation.

(4) Employee—The term *employee* means an individual employed by an employer.

(5) Employer—

(A) In general, the term *employer* means a person engaged in an industry affecting commerce who has 15 or more employees for each working day in each of 20 or more calendar weeks in the current or preceding calendar year, and any agent of such person, except that, for two years following the effective date of this title, *employer* means a person engaged in an industry affecting commerce who has 25 or more employees for each working day in each of 20 or more calendar weeks in the current or preceding year, and any agent of such person.

    (B) Exceptions—the term *employer* does not include

        (i) the United States, a corporation wholly owned by the government of the United States, or an Indian tribe; or

        (ii) a bona fide private membership club (other than a labor organization) that is exempt from taxation under Section 501(c) of the Internal Revenue Code of 1986.

AGE DISCRIMINATION ACT 29 U.S.C. § 621 (§ 623)

(a) It shall be unlawful for an employer

    (1) to fail or refuse to hire or to discharge any individual or otherwise discriminate against any individual with respect to his compensation, terms, conditions, or privileges of employment, because of such individual's age. . . .

(c) It shall be unlawful for a labor organization

    (1) to exclude or to expel from its membership, or otherwise to discriminate against, any individual because of his age. . . .

    (3) to cause or attempt to cause an employer to discriminate against an individual in violation of this section. . . .

(f) It shall not be unlawful for an employer, employment agency, or labor organization

    (1) to take any action otherwise prohibited under subsections (a), (b), (c), or (e) of this section where age is a bona fide occupational qualification reasonably necessary to the normal operation of the particular business, or where the differentiation is based on reasonable factors other than age. . . .

    (3) to discharge or otherwise discipline an individual for good cause. . . .

REHABILITATION ACT OF 1973—29 U.S.C. § 794 (§ 504)

The act provides, in part, that

    "No otherwise qualified handicapped individual … shall, solely by reason of his handicap, be excluded from the participation in, be denied the benefits of, or be subjected to discrimination under any program or activity receiving Federal financial assistance."

THE FAMILY AND MEDICAL LEAVE ACT OF 1993 PUBLIC LAW 103–3 ENACTED FEBRUARY 5, 1993

An Act

To grant family and temporary medical leave under certain circumstances. Be it enacted by the Senate and House of Representatives of the United States of America in Congress assembled,

SEC. 2. Findings and Purposes.

(a) FINDINGS. Congress finds that

(1) the number of single-parent households and two-parent households in which the single parent or both parents work is increasing significantly;

(2) it is important for the development of children and the family unit that fathers and mothers be able to participate in early childrearing and the care of family members who have serious health conditions;

(3) the lack of employment policies to accommodate working parents can force individuals to choose between job security and parenting;

(4) there is inadequate job security for employees who have serious health conditions that prevent them from working for temporary periods;

(5) due to the nature of the roles of men and women in our society, the primary responsibility for family caretaking often falls on women, and such responsibility affects the working lives of women more than it affects the working lives of men; and

(6) employment standards that apply to one gender only have serious potential for encouraging employers to discriminate against employees and applicants for employment who are of that gender.

(b) PURPOSES. It is the purpose of this act

(1) to balance the demands of the workplace with the needs of families, to promote the stability and economic security of families, and to promote national interests in preserving family integrity;

(2) to entitle employees to take reasonable leave for medical reasons, for the birth or adoption of a child, and for the care of a child, spouse, or parent who has a serious health condition;

(3) to accomplish the purposes described in paragraphs (1) and (2) in a manner that accommodates the legitimate interests of employers;

(4) to accomplish the purposes described in paragraphs (1) and (2) in a manner that, consistent with the equal protection clause of the Fourteenth Amendment, minimizes the potential for employment discrimination on the basis of sex by ensuring generally that leave is available for eligible medical reasons (including maternity-related disability) and for compelling family reasons, on a gender-neutral basis; and

(5) to promote the goal of equal employment opportunity for women and men, pursuant to such clause.

Glossary of Relevant Legal Terms

abatement termination of a lawsuit.

action a lawsuit proceeding in a court of law.

advisory opinion an opinion generally rendered by a lower court when no actual case is before it.

affidavit a written statement made under oath.

affirm to uphold a lower court's decision or ruling.

allegation a statement usually brought by the plaintiff and expected to be proven in the pleadings of a case.

amicus curiae a friend of the court; a party that does not have a direct interest in a case, but who is requested or offers information to the court to clarify an issue before it.

appeal an application to a higher court to amend or rectify a lower court's ruling.

appellant one who causes an appeal to a higher court; the appellant may be the plaintiff or the defendant.

appellate court a higher court that hears a case on appeal from a lower court.

appellee a person or party against whom an appeal is brought.

arbitrary without a fair and substantial cause.

assault a hostile threat to use physical force.

battery physical contact with another person in a violent, rude, and hostile fashion.

bona fide honestly and in good faith; authentic.

breach failure to execute a legal duty.

brief a written argument presented to a court by attorney(s).

case law a body of law created by the compilation of decisions of the judicial branch of government.

cause of action the basis for a legal challenge.

certiorari a judicial process whereby a case is moved from a lower court to a higher one for review. The record of all proceedings at the lower court is sent to the higher court.

civil action an action in court with the express purpose of gaining or recovering individual or civil rights.

civil rights the personal freedoms of citizens guaranteed by the Thirteenth and Fourteenth Amendments to the U.S. Constitution.

class action legal action brought by one or more individuals on behalf of themselves and others who are affected by a particular issue.

code a systematic compilation of statutes, usually arranged into chapters and headings for convenient access.

common law a system of law in which legal principles are derived from usage and custom as expressed by the courts.

compensatory damages damages awarded to compensate an injured party for actual losses or harm incurred.

complaint a formal plea to a court seeking relief and informing the defendant of the basis for a legal challenge.

concurring opinion an opinion written by a judge expressing the will of the majority in a court ruling.

consent decree agreement by parties to a dispute and the admission by parties that the decree is a just determination of their rights according to the facts related to the case.

contract a legal agreement between parties involving an offer by one side and acceptance by the other side to perform certain duties that are enforceable by courts of law.

contributory negligence the degree of negligence, on the part of the injured party, that when combined with the negligence of the defendant resulted in the proximate cause of the injury.

court of record a court that maintains permanent records of its proceedings.

damages compensation or indemnity claimed by the plaintiff or ordered by the courts for injuries sustained resulting from wrongful acts of the defendant.

declaratory relief an opinion expressed by the court without ordering that anything be done; it recognizes the rights of the parties involved.

decree an order issued by a court in an equity suit.

defamation scandalous words or expression, written or spoken, that result in damages to another's reputation and for which legal action may be taken by the damaged party.

defendant the party against whom a legal action is brought.

deposition a statement of a witness taken under oath and obtained before the actual trial.

discretionary power the authority to exercise judgment in deciding whether to take action in a certain situation.

discrimination the unfair treatment of a group of people by another because of race, gender, religion, culture, national origin or sexual preference.

dissenting opinion an opinion written by a judge in disagreement with the decision of the majority hearing a case.

due process a course of legal proceedings in accordance with principles of law designed to protect individual rights.

emancipation legal release from another's control (married child from parents).

enjoin to require an individual by writ of injunction to perform or refrain from a certain act.

felony a crime punishable by imprisonment or death.

fiduciary a special relationship between individuals in which one person acts for another in a position of trust.

finding the conclusion reached by a court regarding a factual question.

functional exclusion the condition of students with disabilities who are provided equal access to public education by being physically exposed to the same experience as students without disabilities, but without the special provisions that would enable them to benefit from instruction.

governmental function a function that is required of an agency for the protection and welfare of the general public.

hearing an examination of a legal or factual issue by a court.

holding a ruling or decision by the courts on a question or issue properly raised in a case.

implied suggested; not expressed.

in loco parentis in place of parents.

injunction a court order prohibiting a person from committing an act that threatens or may result in injury to another.

invitee a person who is on the property of another by express invitation.

judgment a decision reached by a court.

liable bound or obligated by law; responsible for actions that may require restitution.

licensee a person granted the privilege to enter into property by actual or implied consent for his or her own purpose rather than the purpose of the one who owns the property.

litigation formal challenge involving a dispute in a court; a lawsuit.

malfeasance commission of an unlawful act.

malice the intentional commission of a wrongful act without justification.

mandate a legal command.

material recognized by the court as important to a case.

ministerial acts actions required, usually by public officials, in which there is no discretion.

misfeasance improper performance of a lawful act.

motion a request for a court ruling.

negligence a lack of proper care; failure to exercise prudence, which may result in injury to another.

nuisance a condition that restricts the use of property or creates a potentially dangerous situation for the user.

original jurisdiction the legal capacity of a court to accept a case at its inception.

parens patriae the state's guardianship over those unable to direct their own affairs, e.g., minors.

petition a written application to a court for the redress of a wrong or the grant of a privilege or license.

plaintiff the party who brings action by filing a complaint.

pleadings formal documents filed in court containing the plaintiff's contention and the defendant's response.

plenary full; complete.

police powers the inherent powers of the government to impose restrictions to protect the health, safety, and welfare of its citizens.

precedent a decision relied on for subsequent decisions in addressing similar or identical questions of law.

prima facie at first view; presumed to be true if not rebutted or proven untrue.

proprietary function a function not normally required by statutes or law and usually involving a state or governmental agent.

punitive damages an award intended to punish the wrongdoer.

quid pro quo a consideration; giving one valuable thing in exchange for another.

relief legal redress sought in the court by the plaintiff.

remand to send back; the act of an appellate court when it sends a case back to the lower court for further proceedings.

remedy a court's enforcement of a right or the prevention of the violation of such right.

respondeat superior the responsibility of a master for the acts of his servants.

respondent the party against whom an appeal is taken; the defendant.

restrain to prevent or prohibit from action.

slander oral defamation.

sovereign immunity a doctrine providing immunity from a lawsuit of a governmental body without its express consent.

standing the right to raise an issue in a lawsuit.

stare decisis to stand by a decided case.

statute an act of the state or federal legislative body; a law.

statute of limitations a statute that establishes the period during which litigation may be initiated in a particular cause of action.

substantive law the proper law of rights and duties.

suit a proceeding in a court of law, initiated by the plaintiff.

summary judgment a court's decision to settle a dispute or dispose of a case promptly without conducting full legal proceedings.

tenure a security measure for those who successfully perform duties and meet statutory or contractual requirements; a continuous service contract.

tort An actionable wrong committed against another independent of contract; a civil wrong.

trespass the unauthorized entry upon the property of another; taking or interfering with the property of another.

vacate to rescind a court decision.

vested fixed; not subject to any contingency.

vicarious liability a form of liability in which school districts are held accountable for negligent or intentional wrongdoing of their employees when the act is committed within the scope of the district employment position, even though the district may not directly be at fault.

void null; without force or a binding effect.

waiver to forgo, renounce, or relinquish a legal right.

warrant a written order of the court; arrest order.

writ of mandamus a command from a court directing a court, officer, or body to perform a certain act.

Index